THE
PUMPKIN SPICE
COOKBOOK

**WHEN USING KITCHEN APPLIANCES PLEASE ALWAYS
FOLLOW THE MANUFACTURER'S INSTRUCTIONS**

HarperCollins*Publishers*
1 London Bridge Street
London SE1 9GF

www.harpercollins.co.uk

HarperCollins*Publishers*
Macken House, 39/40 Mayor Street Upper
Dublin 1, D01 C9W8, Ireland

First published by HarperCollins*Publishers* 2023

1 3 5 7 9 10 8 6 4 2

Text © Heather Thomas 2023
Photography © Sophie Fox 2023

Heather Thomas asserts the moral right to be identified as the author of this work

A catalogue record of this book is available from the British Library

ISBN 978-0-00-862211-4

Photographer: Sophie Fox
Food Stylist: Pippa Leon
Prop Stylist: Faye Wears

Printed and bound in Latvia

THE
PUMPKIN
SPICE
COOKBOOK

60 Wonderfully Warming Recipes

HEATHER THOMAS

HarperCollins*Publishers*

CONTENTS

///

INTRODUCTION

///

Pumpkin spice has seen a huge jump in popularity and sales worldwide in recent years. So much so that it's gone way beyond a traditional autumnal (fall) flavouring in the United States to a worldwide culinary phenomenon. It can now be enjoyed all year-round, not just in lattes and pumpkin pies but also in cakes, desserts, sweet treats, snacks and other savoury dishes.

What is pumpkin spice?

It's an American ground spice mix, which was traditionally used to flavour sweet pumpkin pies eaten at Thanksgiving and Halloween. The most common ingredients are cinnamon, nutmeg, cloves and ginger but sometimes other spices are added, such as cardamom, mace and allspice. You can buy it ready-ground or, better still, grind the spices yourself and make your own more potent mix to suit your personal taste.

History and origins

Pumpkin spice was unknown before the late eighteenth century when the 'Spice Islands' (Indonesia and Malaysia) of Southeast Asia became regular fixtures on American trade routes. Consequently, the early colonists started using the spices to add flavour to sweet as well as savoury food. The native pumpkins were harvested in October and November and the orange flesh was made into sweet pies for their annual Thanksgiving dinner, enhanced by a special blend of warming exotic spices.

The appeal of pumpkin spice

So why do people love pumpkin spice so much? Over the years a great deal of research has been carried out into why the spice is so popular. It seems that most of us associate it with the arrival of autumn and the change in the seasons from the heat and light of summer to cooler weather. As the nights draw in and the colour of the foliage on the trees changes from green to flame red, orange and gold, we crave warmth, roaring fires and comfort food. According to psychologists, the medial temporal lobe in our brain has learned to connect the flavour and aroma of pumpkin spice with the arrival of autumn and images of glowing orange pumpkins piled up on decks and porches, cosy family gatherings and nostalgia. It has a very positive and powerful 'feel-good' effect, making it the ultimate mood food.

And for many men, it is perceived as sexy and an aphrodisiac. Scientific studies have shown that the sweet and spicy aroma of pumpkin spice can drive some mad with desire! Chicago's Smell & Taste Treatment & Research Foundation discovered that men were more turned on by the fragrance of pumpkin spice than by any other smell.

Nutritional benefits

Pumpkin spice is much more than just a delicious, sweet flavouring and aroma. It's comforting, calming, reassuring and warming. And it's packed with antioxidants that help to control our blood sugar levels as well as being a good source of healthy minerals, including iron, manganese, potassium, calcium, zinc and magnesium plus dietary fibre and vitamins C and D. It may also help to relieve digestive problems and improve our brain health, as it possesses anti-inflammatory qualities.

Variety

Best of all, pumpkin spice is wonderfully versatile and can enhance the taste, appearance and aroma of so many foods and dishes, from hot drinks, sweet cakes, cookies, desserts and fruit to savoury snacks, vegetables, dips and chilli. The recipes in this book reflect its incredible variety and range, including basic recipes for syrup, whipped cream, pumpkin spread and frosting. It is often used in conjunction with pumpkin purée, especially for baking and desserts. You can make your own pumpkin purée – in bulk in the autumn when pumpkins are in season and plentiful (it freezes well) – or you can buy it readymade in tins.

Homemade versus commercial pumpkin spice

You can buy readymade pumpkin spice in most supermarkets, delis and wholefood stores as well as online. However, by mixing your own you can adjust the ratio of different ground spices to create the perfect blend. It's cheaper, too, and more flavoursome if you add freshly grated nutmeg, ground cinnamon and cloves. And you can add hints of more unusual spices, such as cardamom, star anise and mace or some hot black pepper or even a dash of chilli. Experiment with different combinations to discover what you like best.

Storage and longevity

Store pumpkin spice in an airtight screw-top glass jar (you can use a funnel to fill the jar) and keep in a cool, dry, dark place, such as a cupboard or pantry. If you use fresh spices, it should stay fresh for up to 12 months. If purchasing ready-ground spices to create your own mix, always check that they are not near or past their expiry date.

BASIC
RECIPES

HOMEMADE PUMPKIN SPICE MIX

//

The classic pumpkin spice is made with ground cinnamon, nutmeg, ginger and cloves. Of course, you can buy it ready-made but making it yourself will create a fresher tasting and more aromatic mixture for flavouring drinks, cakes, desserts, snacks and even savoury dishes. This recipe is not made in tablets of stone, so feel free to adjust the ratio of spices or even to substitute one for another (but not the cinnamon) according to your personal preferences.

MAKES ABOUT 3 TBSP
PREP 5 MINUTES

6 tsp ground cinnamon
2 tsp ground (or finely grated) nutmeg
2 tsp ground ginger
1 tsp ground cloves

Put all the ingredients in a small bowl and mix together well. The ginger sometimes has a tendency to clump but using a wire whisk and then sifting the mixture through a fine sieve will prevent this.

Transfer to an airtight screw-top glass jar (you can use a funnel to fill the jar) and store in a cool, dry, dark place. It will stay fresh for up to 12 months.

Tips: If you are a big fan of pumpkin spice, just double or quadruple the quantity and store it in a larger jar.

Make sure the ground spices you use are as fresh as possible for maximum potency and flavour and not near to or past their expiry date.

Stir the pumpkin spice mix into a jar of caster (superfine) sugar and use in drinks or to sprinkle over pies and cakes.

Variations
· Add ½ teaspoon ground allspice to the mix.
· Add ½ teaspoon ground cardamom.
· For a pungent spice mix, add a pinch of ground black pepper.
· Add a pinch of ground mace or star anise.

PUMPKIN SPICE BUTTER SPREAD

//

You can make a delicious, intensely flavoured pumpkin spice butter for spreading on toasted bread and English muffins, crackers, waffles and scones. You can even add a dollop to a bowl of porridge, granola or yoghurt or stir it into a latte or smoothie. The good news for vegans is that it's plant-based and dairy-free.

**MAKES ABOUT 450G
(1LB/2 CUPS) SPREAD
PREP 5 MINUTES
COOK 35 MINUTES**

850g (1lb 14oz/3½ cups)
   Pumpkin Purée (see page 21)
120ml (4fl oz/½ cup) maple
   syrup
180ml (6fl oz/¾ cup) apple juice
   or cider
2 tsp Pumpkin Spice Mix
   (see page 15)
½ tsp sea salt
2 tsp vanilla extract
2 cinnamon sticks

Put all the ingredients in a saucepan and stir well with a wooden spoon until combined.

Set the pan over a medium to high heat and, stirring occasionally, bring to the boil. As soon as it boils, reduce the heat to low to medium and simmer gently, stirring occasionally, for 30 minutes, or until thickened.

Set aside to cool and remove and discard the cinnamon sticks. Transfer to an airtight container, such as a screw-top glass jar. The spread will keep well in the fridge for 3–4 weeks.

Variations
• Use 200g (7oz/1 cup) soft light brown sugar instead of maple syrup.
• For a super spicy flavour, use 3 teaspoons pumpkin spice mix.

PUMPKIN SPICE WHIPPED CREAM

///

Fragrantly spiced, billowing whipped cream is a great accompaniment to fruit, waffles, cakes and desserts as well as a topping for lattes, cappuccinos and milkshakes. You can also use it to sandwich meringues, fill coffee iced éclairs and top pavlovas. To make this, you will need either a stand food mixer or a hand-held electric whisk.

**MAKES 300ML
(½ PINT/1¼ CUPS) CREAM
PREP 5–10 MINUTES**

300ml (½ pint/1¼ cups) double (heavy) or whipping cream
2 tbsp icing (confectioner's) sugar
1 tsp Pumpkin Spice Mix (see page 15)
½ tsp vanilla extract

Tips: For the best results, chill the bowl and whisk or beaters in advance and use cold cream straight from the fridge.

Do not over-whip the cream or it will lose its silky texture and become grainy.

If you are using a hand-held electric whisk, put the cream, sugar, pumpkin spice and vanilla extract in a bowl and whip until the cream forms stiff peaks and the whisk holds a trail when you lift it out of the mixture.

Alternatively, beat the ingredients together in the bowl of a stand food mixer fitted with the whisk attachment. Start on medium speed and when the cream thickens, increase the speed to high. Keep whipping until it stands in stiff peaks and the whisk holds a trail when you lift it out of the mixture.

Use immediately or store in a covered container in the fridge for up to 2 days.

Variations
- Use grated orange zest instead of vanilla extract.
- For a special occasion, add a few drops of bourbon or amaretto liqueur.

PUMPKIN SPICE SYRUP

//

Make your own pumpkin spice syrup to flavour lattes and to drizzle over ice cream, pancakes, waffles, French toast and cakes.

**MAKES 240ML (8FL OZ/
1 CUP) SYRUP**
PREP 5 MINUTES
COOK 10 MINUTES

225g (8oz/1 cup) caster
   (superfine) sugar
85g (3oz/⅓ cup) Pumpkin Purée
   (see page 21)
1 tsp ground ginger
1 tsp ground cinnamon
¼ tsp ground cloves
a good pinch of grated nutmeg
½ tsp vanilla extract
240ml (8fl oz/1 cup) water

Put all the ingredients in a saucepan and set over a medium heat.

Cook, stirring occasionally with a wooden spoon, for 10 minutes, or until the sugar has dissolved and the mixture is syrupy and coats the back of the spoon.

Take the pan off the heat and set aside to cool. When it's cold, pour into a sterilized screw-top glass jar or bottle. Store in the fridge and use within 3–4 weeks.

Variations
- You can vary the spices according to your personal preference.
- For a darker syrup, use soft light brown sugar.
- For a more pronounced pumpkin flavour, you can add a little more purée.

PUMPKIN SPICE BUTTERCREAM FROSTING

///

This recipe makes enough buttercream frosting to top 12 cupcakes or muffins or sandwich together and top two 18cm (7 inch) sponge cakes. You can spread it with a palette knife or use it to fill a piping (pastry) bag and pipe it in rosettes or stars.

MAKES ABOUT 400G (14OZ/ 2½ CUPS) FROSTING
PREP 5–10 MINUTES

100g (3½oz/scant ½ cup) softened unsalted butter
100g (3½oz/scant 1 cup) icing (confectioner's) sugar, sifted
1–2 tsp Pumpkin Spice Mix (see page 15)
1 tsp vanilla extract
200g (7oz/scant 1 cup) cream cheese (at room temperature)

Put the butter, icing sugar, pumpkin spice mix and vanilla extract in a bowl and, starting on a low speed, mix gently with a hand-held electric whisk. Alternatively, use a stand food mixer.

Increase the speed and beat until the mixture is blended and pale, fluffy and smooth.

Add the cream cheese and continue whisking until well blended, thick and creamy. Taste, adding more pumpkin spice, if liked.

Use immediately or cover the bowl and keep in the fridge for 1–2 days.

Variations
• Add 2 tablespoons pumpkin purée (see opposite) for flavour and colour.
• Instead of vanilla, add some grated orange zest.

PUMPKIN PURÉE

//

Many of the recipes in this book call for pumpkin purée and, although you can buy it in tins and jars in most delis and supermarkets, it's good to make your own when pumpkins are in season and plentiful. It freezes well so you can always have a supply of your delicious homemade version.

**MAKES ABOUT 1–1.5KG
(2¼–3¼LB/4–6 CUPS) PURÉE
PREP 10 MINUTES
COOK 40–60 MINUTES**

1 small pumpkin (about
1.8–3kg/4–6¾lb)

Tip: If you don't have a food processor, you can make the purée in batches in a blender.

Preheat the oven to 200°C (180°C fan)/400°F/gas 6. Line a large baking tray with baking parchment.

Cut the pumpkin in half and scoop out and discard all the seeds and any stringy flesh. Place the two halves, cut-side down, on the lined baking tray.

Bake for 40–60 minutes, or until you can easily pierce the outer skin with a skewer and the flesh is soft and tender and coming away from the skin. Remove from the oven and set aside to cool.

When the pumpkin is cool enough to handle, peel away the skin and transfer the flesh to a food processor. Blitz until you have a really smooth purée. Check the texture of the purée – it should not be watery. You want it to be similar to that of tinned pumpkin purée. If it's too watery, just spoon it into a fine-mesh sieve (strainer) lined with some muslin (cheesecloth) and set it over a large bowl to catch any excess water.

Transfer the purée to a sealed container and keep in the fridge for up to 7 days or store in the freezer for up to 3 months.

Variations
· If you want to use the purée in savoury dishes, you can season it with sea salt to taste.
· Make a butternut squash purée in the same way.

BRUNCHES, SNACKS AND TREATS

PUMPKIN SPICE FRENCH TOAST

//

Pumpkin spice and purée give a lovely warm autumnal flavour to crisply fried French toast. For the best results don't use fresh bread, which will soak up the batter and go soggy. Cut the slices from a firm day-old loaf.

SERVES 4
PREP 5 MINUTES
COOK 12–18 MINUTES

3 medium free-range eggs
120ml (4fl oz/½ cup) milk
50g (2oz/¼ cup) Pumpkin Purée
    (see page 21)
1½ tsp Pumpkin Spice Mix
    (see page 15)
1 tsp granulated sugar
a pinch of sea salt
2 tbsp unsalted butter
8 thick slices bread or brioche
maple syrup, for drizzling
icing (confectioner's) sugar,
    for dusting
crispy bacon or pancetta,
    to serve

Beat together the eggs and milk in a bowl. Add the pumpkin purée, pumpkin spice mix, sugar and salt and whisk until well combined.

Melt half the butter in a large non-stick frying pan (skillet) set over a medium heat.

Dip the slices of bread, one at a time, into the batter, soaking it for a few seconds to absorb the liquid. Let any excess batter drip off the bread into the bowl.

Add the bread to the hot pan, in batches (depending on how many slices the pan can hold), and cook for 2–3 minutes, or until golden brown and crisp underneath. Turn the bread over and cook the other side for 2–3 minutes. Remove from the pan and cook the remaining bread in the same way, adding more butter as required.

Serve the French toast immediately, drizzled with maple syrup and dusted with icing sugar, with some crispy bacon or pancetta on the side.

Variations
- Use plant-based milk, e.g. almond, instead of dairy.
- Substitute vegetable or olive oil for the butter.
- Add 1 teaspoon vanilla extract to the batter.

SPICY YOGHURT AND AUTUMN FRUIT

//

Why not try a dish of stewed fruit with lightly spiced creamy yoghurt for breakfast or brunch or enjoy it as a healthy snack or dessert? In the summer, you can substitute peaches, cherries and soft fruits for the apples, plums and blackberries.

SERVES 4
PREP 10 MINUTES
COOK 10–12 MINUTES

50g (2oz/¼ cup) butter
50g (2oz/¼ cup) caster (superfine) or soft light brown sugar
3 dessert (sweet) apples, peeled, cored and thickly sliced
450g (1lb) ripe plums or greengages, stoned (pitted) and quartered
1 tsp Pumpkin Spice Mix (see page 15)
250g (9oz) blackberries

PUMPKIN SPICED YOGHURT

400g (14oz/1¾ cups) Greek yoghurt
½ tsp Pumpkin Spice Mix (see page 15)
a good pinch of ground cinnamon
maple syrup or honey, to sweeten (optional)

Melt the butter in a large frying pan (skillet) set over a low to medium heat. Stir in the sugar and when it dissolves and starts to foam, add the apples and plums.

Cook gently, stirring occasionally, for 6–8 minutes, or until the apples are soft and golden and the plums or greengages are tender. Stir in the pumpkin spice mix and the blackberries and simmer gently for 2 minutes until the juice comes out of the blackberries and colours the mixture.

In a bowl, blend the Greek yoghurt with the pumpkin spice mix and cinnamon. If wished, sweeten to taste with maple syrup or honey.

Serve the stewed autumn fruit warm or at room temperature with a large dollop of pumpkin-spiced yoghurt.

Tip: You can keep any leftover stewed fruit or spiced yoghurt in sealed containers in the fridge for up to 3 days.

Variations
· Substitute quinces or pears for the apples.
· Use peaches instead of plums or greengages.
· Add some stoned (pitted) dark cherries.
· Add some grated orange zest to the yoghurt.
· Drizzle with honey and sprinkle with toasted nuts.

PUMPKIN SPICE BREAKFAST PANCAKES

What could be more delicious for breakfast than warmly spiced fluffy pancakes drizzled with maple syrup? Adding pumpkin spice and purée transforms a pancake batter into something truly special.

MAKES 8–10 PANCAKES
PREP 10 MINUTES
COOK 25–30 MINUTES

2 large free-range eggs
200ml (7fl oz/scant 1 cup)
  semi-skimmed milk
115g (4oz/½ cup) Pumpkin Purée
  (see page 21)
1 tsp vanilla extract
5 tbsp vegetable oil, plus extra
  for brushing
200g (7oz/2 cups) plain
  (all-purpose) flour
2 tsp baking powder
3 tbsp caster (superfine) sugar
2 tsp Pumpkin Spice Mix
  (see page 15)
½ tsp sea salt
maple syrup, for drizzling

Tip: You could use two frying pans to cut the cooking time.

In a bowl, beat the eggs, milk, pumpkin purée, vanilla extract and oil until well blended.

Sift the flour and baking powder into a large bowl and stir in the sugar, pumpkin spice mix and salt. Make a well in the centre and pour in the beaten egg mixture. Stir gently until everything is well combined but be careful not to over-mix. Transfer to a measuring jug.

Set a large frying pan (skillet) over a medium to high heat and lightly brush with oil. When it's really hot, add a small ladle of the batter to the pan. When bubbles appear on the surface and the edges start to brown after 1–2 minutes, flip the pancake over and cook for 1–2 minutes until set and browned underneath. Remove and keep warm while you make the rest of the pancakes in the same way.

Serve the pancakes piping hot and drizzled with maple syrup.

Variations
- For even more fluffy pancakes, substitute buttermilk for the milk.
- Serve with chopped pecans and some whipped cream.

PUMPKIN SPICE DIPPERS

//

These sweet and spicy dippers are great for parties or to serve with dips as a fun dessert. You don't need to spend time making croissant or pastry dough – just use a tube of ready-made chilled dough from the supermarket.

MAKES ABOUT 12 TWISTS
PREP 15 MINUTES
COOK 8-10 MINUTES

115g (4oz/½ cup) Pumpkin Purée
(see page 21)
2 tsp Pumpkin Spice Mix
(see page 15)
50g (2oz/¼ cup) soft light brown
sugar
1 chilled tube croissant (crescent
roll) dough (about 350g/12oz)
2–3 tbsp melted butter

PUMPKIN SPICE SPRINKLE
1 tbsp caster (superfine) sugar
1 tsp Pumpkin Spice Mix
(see page 15)

Preheat the oven to 200°C (180°C fan)/400°F/gas 6. Line a baking tray with baking parchment.

Make the pumpkin spice sprinkle by mixing the sugar and spice mix in a bowl.

Mix together the pumpkin purée, spice mix and sugar in a separate bowl.

Unroll the croissant dough and cut into four rectangles. Spread the pumpkin purée mixture over two rectangles and place the other two pieces of dough on top, pressing the edges of the dough together to seal them.

Cut each rectangle lengthways into long, thin strips – use a pizza cutter if you have one. Twist each strip once or twice at each end and place on the lined baking tray. Brush with melted butter and dust with the pumpkin spice sprinkle.

Bake for 8–10 minutes until crisp and golden. Eat warm on their own or dipped into a bowl of melted dark chocolate or pumpkin spice whipped cream (see page 17).

Variations
• Substitute cinnamon for the pumpkin spice in the sprinkle.
• Use agave or maple syrup instead of brown sugar.
• Use ready-made puff pastry sheets instead of croissant dough.

PUMPKIN SPICE GRANOLA

//

There are no hard-and-fast rules about what you put into this delicious vegan granola. Just use whatever you've got to hand – walnuts, pecans, almonds, chopped dates, dried cranberries, etc. Serve the granola with milk or yoghurt topped with any seasonal fruit and drizzle with maple or Pumpkin Spice Syrup (see page 18) or some clear honey.

MAKES 8 SERVINGS
PREP 10 MINUTES
COOK 20–25 MINUTES

60g (2oz/4 tbsp) coconut oil
4 tbsp maple syrup
200g (7oz/2½ cups) rolled oats
85g (3oz/generous ½ cup)
  chopped hazelnuts
25g (1oz/scant ¼ cup) sunflower
  seeds
50g (2oz/scant ½ cup) pumpkin
  seeds
3 tbsp sesame seeds
100g (3½oz/scant ¾ cup) raisins
1½ tsp Pumpkin Spice Mix
  (see page 15)

Tip: Double or triple the quantities to make a bigger batch.

Preheat the oven to 170°C (150°C fan)/325°F/gas 3. Line a large baking tray with baking parchment.

Heat the coconut oil and maple syrup in a saucepan set over a low heat. When the coconut oil melts, stir in the oats, nuts, seeds, raisins and pumpkin spice mix. Make sure that everything is well coated.

Spread the mixture out in a thin layer on the lined baking tray and bake for 15–20 minutes, stirring once or twice, until golden brown and crisp.

Leave the granola to cool on the baking tray before transferring to an airtight container. It will keep well for up to 2 weeks.

Variations
- Vary the nuts: try chopped walnuts, pecans or almonds.
- Stir in some dried cranberries or blueberries after baking.
- For extra flavour add a few drops of vanilla extract.
- Add some chocolate chips once the granola has cooled.
- Add 1–2 tbsp Pumpkin Purée (see page 21) to the mixture before cooking.

PUMPKIN SPICE WAFFLES

///

These delicately spiced pumpkin waffles are perfect for a weekend breakfast or brunch. You will need a waffle iron to make them. Please note that the batter should be used as soon as it is made.

MAKES 8-10 WAFFLES
PREP 15 MINUTES
COOK 15-20 MINUTES

150g (5oz/1½ cups) plain (all-purpose) flour
2 tsp baking powder
½ tsp sea salt
2 tsp Pumpkin Spice Mix (see page 15)
2 tbsp soft light brown sugar
2 large free-range eggs, beaten
240ml (8fl oz/1 cup) unsweetened almond milk (or milk of your choice)
115g (4oz/¼ cup) Pumpkin Purée (see page 21)
1 tsp vanilla extract
3 tbsp melted butter
spray oil
maple syrup and coconut yoghurt, to serve

Sift the flour, baking powder and salt into a large bowl and stir in the pumpkin spice mix and sugar.

In another bowl, mix together the beaten eggs, milk, pumpkin purée, vanilla and melted butter.

Tip in the flour mixture and stir until just combined. Do not over-mix the batter – it does not matter if there are a few small lumps.

Preheat a waffle iron and lightly spray with oil – if you have a non-stick waffle iron, there's no need to do this. Ladle in some of the batter, then seal and follow the manufacturer's instructions until cooked, crisp and golden brown. Keep warm while you cook the remaining waffles in the same way.

Serve the hot waffles drizzled with maple syrup and topped with the coconut yoghurt.

Variations
· Dust the hot waffles with icing (confectioner's) sugar.
· Serve with apple purée, spiced with cinnamon.
· Sprinkle with toasted nuts.
· Drizzle with salted caramel sauce and add whipped cream.
· Go savoury and eat the waffles with crispy bacon and maple syrup.

Tips: Adding pumpkin purée can make the waffles a little soft in the centre, so you may wish to use the medium-high setting on your waffle maker.

PUMPKIN SPICE BREAKFAST BARS

///

These crunchy bars are so easy to make and perfect for breakfast on-the-go or
as a pick-me-up during the day.

MAKES 12 BARS
PREP 15 MINUTES
COOK 25–30 MINUTES

300g (10oz/3¼ cups) rolled oats
75g (3oz/scant ¾ cup) chopped
    pecans or walnuts
100g (3½oz/scant ¾ cup) ready-
    to-eat dried apricots, chopped
85g (3oz/generous ¼ cup)
    stoned (pitted) dates, chopped
50g (2oz/generous ½ cup) dried
    cranberries or blueberries
50g (2oz/scant ½ cup) raisins
4 tbsp mixed seeds, e.g.
    pumpkin, sunflower, chia
2 tsp Pumpkin Spice Mix
    (see page 15)
a good pinch of sea salt
150g (5oz/generous ½ cup)
    butter, plus extra for greasing
6 tbsp maple syrup
1 tsp vanilla extract

Preheat the oven to 170°C (150°C fan)/325°F/gas 3. Lightly
butter a 30 x 20cm (12 x 8 inch) baking tin (pan) and line with
baking parchment.

Put the oats, nuts, dried fruits, seeds, pumpkin spice mix and salt
in a large mixing bowl.

Put the butter and maple syrup in a saucepan set over a low heat.
Stir gently until the butter melts and blends with the syrup. Add
to the oat mixture with the vanilla extract and mix well. If it's too
dry, add some more melted butter; if it's not firm enough and too
sticky, add more oats.

Transfer to the lined tin and smooth the top. Bake for about
25–30 minutes until crisp and golden brown.

Remove from the oven and cool slightly before cutting into 12
bars. Leave in the tin until completely cold, then remove and
store in an airtight container. They will keep well for up to 5 days.

Variations
• Add some dark chocolate chips.
• Use hazelnuts instead of pecans or walnuts.
• Substitute clear honey or agave for the maple syrup.

Tip: If the mixture
seems dry, you can
moisten it with 1–2
tablespoons pumpkin
purée (see page 21).

PUMPKIN SPICE PRETZELS

//

Delightfully crunchy, sweet and salty, these pumpkin spice pretzels make a great snack. Serve them with drinks or set out a large bowl for a Halloween or Thanksgiving party.

SERVES 6–8
PREP 10 MINUTES
COOK 8–10 MINUTES

90ml (3fl oz/⅓ cup) runny honey
2 tbsp Pumpkin Spice Mix
  (see page 15)
450g (1lb/4 cups) mini pretzels
115g (4oz/½ cup) caster
  (superfine) sugar

Preheat the oven to 180°C (160°C fan)/350°F/gas 4. Line a rimmed large baking tray with baking parchment.

Put the honey and pumpkin spice in a microwave-safe bowl and microwave on High for 30 seconds. Add the mini pretzels to the bowl and stir gently until coated all over.

Spread the coated pretzels out on the lined baking tray in a single layer and bake for 8–10 minutes.

Remove and, while the pretzels are still hot, sprinkle with the sugar. Toss gently until the pretzels are evenly coated. Set aside to cool before eating. They will keep well stored in an airtight container for 3–4 weeks.

Variations
· Drizzle with some melted white chocolate.
· Use maple syrup instead of honey.
· Try stirring some chopped pecans, dried cranberries or toasted pumpkin seeds into the pumpkin spice pretzels before serving.

SPICY PUMPKIN SEED SNACK

//

It's always a good idea to have a supply of these delicious crunchy pumpkin seeds to hand. Eat them as a snack, serve with drinks or sprinkle them over your breakfast oatmeal or yoghurt. They are the perfect way to use up the seeds in a large Halloween pumpkin – nothing gets thrown away or wasted!

**MAKES 250G
(9OZ/2 CUPS) SNACKS
PREP 15 MINUTES
COOK 35-40 MINUTES**

250g (9oz/2 cups) raw fresh
   pumpkin seeds
2 tbsp olive oil
2 tsp Pumpkin Spice Mix
   (see page 15)
1 tbsp white sugar or maple syrup
½ tsp sea salt (optional)

Preheat the oven to 170°C (150°C fan)/325°F/gas 3. Line a large baking tray with kitchen paper (kitchen towel).

Scrape the pumpkin seeds out of the pumpkin and remove any stringy flesh and pulp.

Rinse the seeds in a colander under cold running water. Drain well and then spread them out on the lined baking tray. Set aside and leave to dry.

Toss the dry seeds in the olive oil and pumpkin spice mix with the sugar or maple syrup, then spread them out in a single layer on a rimmed large baking tray. Roast, turning two or three times, for 35–40 minutes, or until golden brown.

Remove from the oven, sprinkle with salt (optional) and set aside to cool. Store in an airtight container at room temperature. The seeds will stay fresh for up to 2 weeks.

Variations
- Use coconut oil instead of olive oil.
- Add extra ground cinnamon and a grinding of black pepper.
- Instead of adding the sugar or syrup before roasting, sprinkle the sugar over the hot roasted seeds.
- Add the toasted seeds to a trail mix.

PUMPKIN SPICE KRISPIE SNACKS

///

These old-school Krispie squares are the perfect treat for a Halloween party. Adults seem to love them as much as children. Plus, they are so easy to make and there's virtually no cooking.

MAKES 9 SQUARES
PREP 10 MINUTES
COOK 6–8 MINUTES
CHILL 1 HOUR

85g (3oz/⅓ cup) butter, plus extra for greasing
50g (2oz/¼ cup) Pumpkin Purée (see page 21)
300g (10oz) mini marshmallows
2 tsp Pumpkin Spice Mix (see page 15)
½ tsp vanilla extract
180g (6oz/6 cups) crispy rice cereal, e.g. Rice Krispies
85g (3oz/½ cup) dark (bittersweet) chocolate chips (minimum 70% cocoa solids)

Tip: When you pour the mixture into the cake tin, do not press it down too hard. You want the cereal to stay crisp and keep its shape.

Generously butter a 23cm (9 inch) square cake tin (baking pan).

Put the butter in a saucepan and set over a low heat. When it melts, stir in the pumpkin purée and cook for 2 minutes until well blended.

Add the marshmallows and stir them through the buttery pumpkin mixture. Cook, stirring occasionally, for 2–3 minutes until they melt. Stir in the pumpkin spice mix and vanilla.

Remove from the heat and set aside for 5 minutes before adding the crispy rice cereal. Fold it in gently until coated all over and distributed throughout the mixture.

Transfer to the buttered cake tin, pushing the mixture into the corners. Use a spatula to gently level the top.

Melt the chocolate in a bowl suspended over a pan of gently simmering water. Drizzle the melted chocolate over the mixture.

Chill in the fridge for 1 hour or until the mixture is firm and set before cutting into squares. Transfer to an airtight container and store in a cool, dry place for up to 5 days.

Variations
· Drizzle with melted white or milk chocolate.
· Top with your favourite buttercream or frosting.
· Add chopped nuts or crumbled pretzels to the mixture.

PUMPKIN SPICE ENERGY BALLS

These bite-sized energy balls are great to snack on when you're feeling peckish and need a quick energy boost. They are very versatile and you can experiment with the ingredients depending on what you've got in your kitchen cupboards.

MAKES ABOUT 30 BALLS
PREP 15 MINUTES
CHILL 2 HOURS

175g (6oz/1 cup) unsweetened almond butter
5 tbsp maple syrup
1 tsp vanilla extract
175g (6oz/1¾ cups) rolled porridge oats
1–2 tsp Pumpkin Spice Mix (see page 15)
30g (1oz/¼ cup) dried cranberries
60g (2oz/generous ¼ cup) dark (bittersweet) chocolate chips (minimum 70% cocoa solids)
finely chopped almonds, for coating

Tips: Vegans can use non-dairy vegan chocolate.

The energy balls will freeze well for up to 3 months.

Line a large baking tray with baking parchment.

Put the almond butter and maple syrup in a saucepan and set over a low heat. Stir gently until just warm and well blended.

Take the pan off the heat and stir in the vanilla extract, oats, pumpkin spice mix (according to taste), cranberries and chocolate chips. If the mixture is too sticky and wet, add some more oats; if it's too dry, mix in a little cold water to moisten it.

Take small spoonfuls of the mixture and shape into bite-sized balls with your hands. Roll them in the chopped almonds until coated all over.

Place the balls on the lined baking tray and chill in the fridge for 2 hours or until firm and set. Transfer to an airtight container and store in the fridge for up to 1 week.

Variations
· Roll the balls in cocoa powder or desiccated coconut.
· Add some chia, flax, sunflower or poppy seeds.
· Stir in 1–2 tablespoons Pumpkin Purée (see page 21).
· Boost the protein content by adding a scoop of protein powder.

PUMPKIN SPICE POPCORN

///

Enjoy this sweet-and-spicy popcorn as a snack or a home movie-night treat. You can use a pack of plain unsalted and unsweetened ready-popped popcorn from the supermarket or make your own.

SERVES 4–5
PREP 5 MINUTES
COOK 2–3 MINUTES

30g (1oz/⅛ cup) popcorn kernels
2 tsp Pumpkin Spice Mix
   (see page 15)
¼ tsp sea salt
2 tbsp butter
2 tbsp maple syrup

Cook the popcorn kernels according to the manufacturer's instructions on the packet. Tip the popped popcorn into a large bowl.

Stir together the pumpkin spice mix and salt in a small bowl.

Melt the butter in a pan set over a low heat and gently stir in the maple syrup.

Drizzle over the popcorn, tossing it gently until coated all over, and then toss in the salty pumpkin spice.

Tip: If there's any leftover popcorn, store it in an airtight container for up to 1 day.

Variations
- Use soft light brown sugar instead of maple syrup.
- Add a couple of drops of vanilla extract.
- Drizzle with salted caramel sauce.

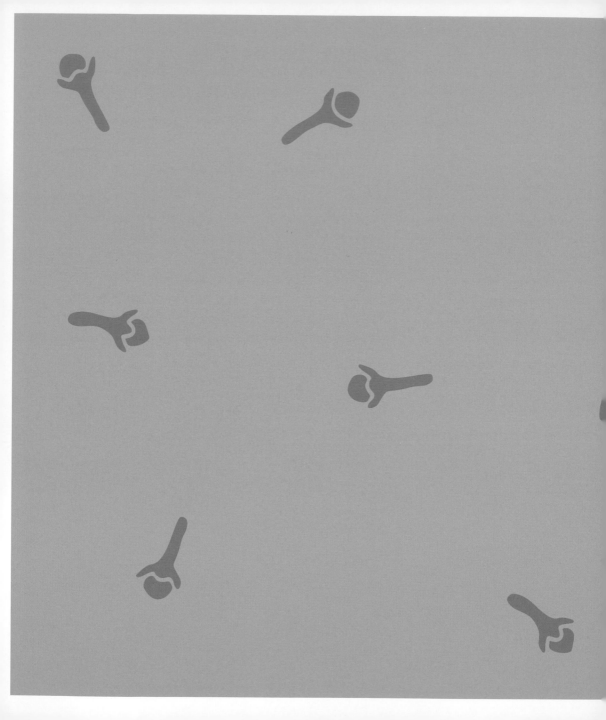

SOUPS AND SAVOURY DISHES

WINTER ROOTS SOUP

///

This is the perfect cold-weather soup – warming, spicy and a good source of vegetable protein and zinc. It will keep in the freezer for up to 3 months, and it's vegan and gluten-free.

SERVES: 4–6
PREP 20 MINUTES
COOK 30–40 MINUTES

2 tbsp olive oil
1 large onion, finely chopped
2 garlic cloves, crushed
1 celery stick, diced
2 large carrots, thinly sliced
1 large parsnip, thinly sliced
900g (2lb) pumpkin, peeled,
   deseeded and cubed
2 potatoes, cubed
3 tsp Pumpkin Spice Mix
   (see page 15)
1 tsp ground turmeric
1.2 litres (2 pints/5 cups) hot
   vegetable stock
400g (14oz) tin butterbeans
   (lima), rinsed and drained
120ml (4fl oz/½ cup) almond
   or oat milk
sea salt and black pepper
chopped parsley, for sprinkling

SPICY ONIONS

2 tbsp olive oil
1 red onion, thinly sliced
2 garlic cloves, crushed
1 red chilli, shredded
1 tsp yellow mustard seeds
1 tsp cumin seeds

Heat the oil in a large saucepan set over a low heat. Cook the onion, garlic, celery, carrots and parsnip, stirring occasionally, for 6–8 minutes, until softened. Add the pumpkin and potato and cook for 5 minutes. Add the spices and cook for 1 minute.

Add the hot stock and bring to the boil, then reduce the heat and simmer gently for 15–20 minutes, or until the vegetables are tender. Add half the beans to the soup.

Meanwhile, make the spicy onions: heat the oil in a frying pan (skillet) set over a low heat and cook the onion, stirring occasionally, for 10 minutes, or until tender and golden brown. Add the garlic, chilli and seeds and increase the heat. Cook for 1–2 minutes until the mustard seeds start popping.

Blitz the soup in a blender or food processor until smooth. Return to the pan and stir in the milk and the rest of the beans. Season to taste with salt and pepper and heat through gently over a low heat.

Ladle the soup into bowls, then sprinkle with parsley and top with the spicy onions. Serve immediately.

Variations
· Use cannellini, haricot beans or chickpeas (garbanzos).
· Sprinkle with grated cheese instead of the spicy onions.
· Vary the vegetables: try butternut squash, celeriac or sweet potato.

SWEET-AND-SPICY BUTTERNUT SQUASH AND LENTIL SOUP

//

The ginger, chilli flakes and coconut milk add some Thai flavourings to this slightly grainy lentil soup, while the pmpkin spice and sweet potatoes infuse it with sweetness and warmth.

SERVES 4-6
PREP 15 MINUTES
COOK 30-35 MINUTES

2 tbsp olive oil
1 large onion, chopped
2 garlic cloves, crushed
2.5cm (1 inch) piece of fresh root
   ginger, peeled and grated
a pinch of crushed dried chilli
   flakes
2 tsp Pumpkin Spice Mix
   (see page 15)
½ tsp ground turmeric
100g (3½oz/½ cup) red lentils
720ml (1¼ pints/3 cups) hot
   vegetable stock
400ml (14fl oz) tin reduced-fat
   coconut milk
400g (14oz) butternut squash,
   peeled, deseeded and cubed
2 large sweet potatoes, peeled
   and cubed
200g (7oz) shredded spinach
   or baby spinach leaves
sea salt and freshly ground
   black pepper
Thai sweet chilli sauce, for
   drizzling

Heat the oil in a large saucepan set over a low to medium heat. Cook the onion, garlic and ginger, stirring occasionally, for about 6–8 minutes, until softened. Stir in the chilli flakes, pumpkin spice mix and turmeric and cook for 1 minute.

Add the lentils and stir well until glistening with oil. Add the stock, coconut milk, squash and sweet potatoes and bring to the boil. Reduce the heat to low and simmer for 15–20 minutes, or until the vegetables are tender.

Transfer half of the soup to a blender or food processor and blitz until smooth. Return to the pan and stir in the spinach. Heat through gently and season to taste with salt and pepper.

Ladle the hot soup into bowls and serve immediately, drizzled with sweet chilli sauce.

Variations
- Use pumpkin instead of squash.
- Instead of spinach, stir in a bunch of chopped coriander (cilantro).
- Flavour with freshly squeezed lime juice.
- Sprinkle with roasted peanuts.

HALLOWEEN PUMPKIN SOUP WITH CHEESY TORTILLAS

//

Serve this smooth and velvety soup in a hollowed-out pumpkin as the centrepiece for Halloween or bonfire night parties. You can make the soup in advance for reheating later, just before filling the pumpkin shell.

SERVES 4–6
PREP 20 MINUTES
COOK 40–45 MINUTES

3 tbsp olive oil
2 large red onions, thinly sliced
2 tsp brown sugar
3 garlic cloves, crushed
1 red chilli, deseeded and diced
2 tsp Pumpkin Spice Mix
    (see page 15)
½ tsp sweet or smoked paprika
1kg (2¼lb) pumpkin, peeled,
    deseeded and cubed
900ml (1½ pints/3¾ cups) hot
    vegetable stock
200ml (7fl oz/scant 1 cup)
    reduced-fat crème fraîche
sea salt and freshly ground
    black pepper

TO SERVE
1 x 2kg (4½lb) pumpkin, hollowed
    out (optional)
chopped coriander (cilantro),
    for sprinkling
crushed dried chilli flakes, for
    sprinkling
100g (3½oz) tortilla chips,
    coarsely crushed
100g (3½oz/1 cup) grated
    Cheddar or Gruyère cheese

Heat the oil in a large saucepan set over a low heat. Add the onion and stir in the sugar. Cook gently, stirring occasionally, for 12–15 minutes, or until golden brown and starting to caramelize.

Add the garlic and chilli and cook for 2 minutes. Stir in the ground spices and pumpkin, pour in the stock and bring to the boil. Reduce the heat and simmer for 20 minutes, or until the pumpkin is cooked.

Blitz in a blender or food processor until smooth. Alternatively, leave in the pan and, off the heat, use a hand-held stick blender.

Gently reheat the soup over a low heat and stir in the crème fraîche. Season to taste with salt and pepper.

Pour the hot soup into the hollowed-out pumpkin shell or ladle into bowls. Sprinkle lightly with coriander and chilli flakes and scatter the tortilla chips and grated cheese over the top.

> **Tip**: if you can't get reduced-fat crème fraîche, just use regular or single (light) cream.

Variations
· Use coconut or almond milk instead of crème fraîche.
· Roast the pumpkin before adding it to the soup.
· Vary the spices: try ground cumin, coriander or turmeric.

PUMPKIN SPICE BAKED SQUASH AND SWEET POTATOES

///

The warming pumpkin spice adds a lovely autumnal flavour and aroma to the sweet and slightly caramelized squash and sweet potatoes. Serve with roast chicken or turkey or a succulent steak. Or mix into a bowl of brown rice, quinoa or crunchy bulgur wheat.

SERVES 4 (AS A SIDE DISH)
PREP 10 MINUTES
COOK 30 MINUTES

500g (1lb 2oz) butternut squash, peeled, deseeded and cubed
500g (1lb 2oz) sweet potatoes, peeled and cubed
6 tbsp olive oil
2 tbsp clear honey
2 tsp Pumpkin Spice Mix (see page 15)
3 tbsp mixed seeds, e.g. cumin, coriander, fennel
seeds of ½ pomegranate
sea salt and freshly ground black pepper

Preheat the oven to 200°C (180°C fan)/400°F/gas 6.

Put the squash and sweet potato in a bowl with the olive oil, honey and pumpkin spice mix. Stir gently until the cubes are lightly coated and glistening with oil.

Place them in a single layer on a large baking tray and season with salt and pepper. Roast for 30 minutes, or until cooked, tender and golden brown.

Meanwhile, set a frying pan (skillet) over a low to medium heat and toast the mixed seeds, stirring occasionally, for 4–5 minutes, or until fragrant and golden. Remove from the pan and crush with a pestle and mortar.

Serve the hot squash and sweet potatoes, sprinkled with the crushed toasted seeds and pomegranate seeds.

Variations
- Substitute pumpkin for the butternut squash.
- Vegans can use maple syrup instead of honey.
- Sprinkle with chopped pistachio nuts.
- Toast some sunflower or pumpkin seeds.
- Drizzle with pomegranate molasses.
- Sprinkle with crushed dried chilli flakes or some finely chopped thyme.

PUMPKIN AND BLACK BEAN CHILLI

///

This veggie pumpkin chilli takes very little time to make and keeps well in an airtight container in the fridge for up to 3 days. Reheat in the microwave and serve with rice, quinoa or bulgur wheat. Vegans can serve this with dairy-free cream or coconut yoghurt.

SERVES 4–6
PREP 15 MINUTES
COOK 25–30 MINUTES

3 tbsp olive oil
2 red onions, thinly sliced
4 garlic cloves, crushed
1 tbsp ground cumin
1 tsp Pumpkin Spice Mix
   (see page 15)
2 tsp chilli powder
500g (1lb 2oz) pumpkin, peeled,
   deseeded and cubed
2 x 400g (14oz) tins chopped
   tomatoes
1 tbsp tomato purée
1 tsp caster (superfine) sugar
400g (14oz) tin black beans,
   rinsed and drained
juice of 1 lime
a handful of coriander (cilantro),
   chopped
sea salt and freshly ground
   black pepper
sour cream, guacamole and lime
   wedges, to serve

Heat the olive oil in a saucepan or a deep frying pan (skillet) set over a low to medium heat and cook the onion and garlic, stirring occasionally, for 10 minutes, or until softened and golden. Stir in the ground spices, chilli powder and pumpkin.

Add the tomatoes, tomato purée, sugar and black beans and cook gently for 15–20 minutes, or until the tomato sauce has thickened and reduced. Season to taste with salt and pepper and stir in the lime juice and most of the coriander.

Divide among four bowls and sprinkle with the remaining coriander. Serve with sour cream and guacamole, plus lime wedges for squeezing

> **Tip**: If the tomato mixture is too thick, thin it with some vegetable stock.

Variations
- Substitute kidney beans for the black beans.
- Add some hot tomato salsa to the sauce.
- Use as a filling for tacos, burritos or wraps.
- Instead of guacamole, serve with diced avocado and grated Cheddar or Monterey Jack cheese.
- Serve with tortilla chips.

ROASTED PUMPKIN HUMMUS

//

This warmly spiced hummus has an appetizing rich golden colour and is the perfect dip to serve as a meze dish, at parties or with pre-dinner drinks. It's delicious with roasted baby carrots, red onion wedges and fennel or just some regular tortilla chips. If you're in a hurry, you can substitute Pumpkin Purée (see page 21) for the roasted pumpkin.

SERVES 6
PREP 15 MINUTES
COOK 20 MINUTES

300g (10oz) pumpkin, peeled, deseeded and cubed
400g (14oz) tin chickpeas (garbanzos)
4 garlic cloves, crushed
1 tsp Pumpkin Spice Mix (see page 15)
½ tsp ground cumin
½ tsp smoked paprika
2 tbsp tahini
juice of 1 lemon, plus extra juice for drizzling
2–3 tbsp olive oil, plus extra for drizzling
sea salt and freshly ground black pepper
toasted pumpkin or pomegranate seeds, for sprinkling

Tip: This keeps well in a sealed container in the fridge for up to 4 days.

Preheat the oven to 200°C (180°C fan)/400°F/gas 6. Place the pumpkin in a single layer on a baking tray and drizzle with olive oil. Roast for 20 minutes or until tender. Set aside to cool.

Drain the chickpeas and reserve the liquid. Rinse the chickpeas in a sieve under running cold water and pat dry with kitchen paper (paper towels).

Blitz the roasted pumpkin, chickpeas, garlic, ground spices, tahini, lemon juice and olive oil in a food processor or blender. If wished, use a little of the reserved chickpea liquid to thin the mixture to the consistency you want. It should be slightly grainy and creamy. Season to taste with salt and pepper.

Transfer to a shallow bowl and drizzle with more olive oil and lemon juice. Sprinkle with toasted pumpkin seeds or pomegranate seeds and serve with crusty bread, crackers, warmed pita or flatbreads or as a dip for tortilla chips or raw or roasted vegetables.

Variations
· Serve sprinkled with dukkah or toasted pine nuts.
· Dust with pumpkin spice mix or hot and spicy cayenne.
· Sprinkle with chopped parsley or coriander (cilantro).
· For a creamier hummus, stir in some 0% fat Greek yoghurt.
· Crumble some feta over the top.

SPICY PUMPKIN DIP

//

This fabulous dip is best served lukewarm with some warmed flatbread or pita triangles for dipping (see tip). It's a variation on the classic Greek fava, which is made with yellow split peas and served as part of a meze spread. You can also serve it as a side dish with grilled fish, meat and chicken.

SERVES 6-8
PREP 15 MINUTES
COOK 45-55 MINUTES

450g (1lb/2 cups) yellow split peas
1 onion, peeled and quartered
2 garlic cloves, peeled
1 bay leaf
a few sprigs of thyme
100ml (3½fl oz/scant ½ cup) fruity
    olive oil, plus extra for drizzling
juice of 1 lemon
115g (4oz/¼ cup) Pumpkin Purée
    (see page 21)
1 tsp Pumpkin Spice Mix
    (see page 15) , plus extra for
    dusting
sea salt and black pepper
finely chopped red onions, capers
    and lemon wedges, to serve

Rinse the split peas in a sieve under running cold water. Put them into a large saucepan with the onion, garlic and herbs. Cover with plenty of cold water and set over a high heat. Bring to the boil and skim off the foamy scum that rises to the surface.

Lower the heat and simmer gently for 40–50 minutes, or until the split peas are very soft and most of the water has been absorbed. Drain in a sieve suspended over a bowl to catch the cooking liquid. Discard the onion and herbs but keep the garlic.

Place the warm split peas and garlic in a blender or food processor. With the motor running, start adding the olive oil through the feed tube in a thin, steady stream, then add the lemon juice, pumpkin purée and pumpkin spice mix. It should have a soft, slightly grainy texture. Season to taste with salt and pepper.

Transfer to a serving bowl, dust with pumpkin spice mix and drizzle with olive oil. Sprinkle the chopped red onion and capers over the top. Serve lukewarm. It keeps well in an airtight container in the fridge for up to 4 days.

Tip: Use warm pita breads or flatbreads, cut into triangles, as dippers. Heat them in a griddle pan or wrap in foil and warm through in a low oven.

Variations
· Dust with paprika or cayenne.
· Sprinkle with diced spring onions (scallions) and lemon juice.
· Top with caramelized onions or red onion chutney.
· Serve with roasted vegetables, crudité dippers, breadsticks or tortilla chips.

PUMPKIN MAC 'N' CHEESE

//

Who doesn't like mac 'n cheese? Adding tender roasted pumpkin and some pumpkin spice mix transforms it into something special. Make this economical family supper on a cold autumn or winter evening and serve with a crisp salad or steamed green vegetables.

SERVES 4
PREP 20 MINUTES
COOK 45–55 MINUTES

600g (1lb 5oz) pumpkin, peeled, deseeded and cubed
olive oil, for drizzling
300g (10oz) macaroni
3 tbsp unsalted butter, plus extra for greasing
1 onion, finely chopped
2 garlic cloves, crushed
50g (2oz/½ cup) plain (all-purpose) flour
500ml (17fl oz/scant 2 cups) milk
1 tsp Dijon mustard
1 tsp Pumpkin Spice Mix (see page 15)
a few sprigs of parsley, finely chopped
100g (3½oz/1 cup) grated Cheddar cheese
a pinch of crushed dried chilli flakes
3–4 tbsp fresh white breadcrumbs
sea salt and freshly ground black pepper

Preheat the oven to 200°C (180°C fan)/400°F/gas 6. Line a baking tray with baking parchment.

Arrange the pumpkin in a single layer on the lined baking tray. Drizzle with oil and sprinkle with salt and pepper. Roast, turning once, for 25–30 minutes, or until tender.

Meanwhile, cook the macaroni according to the instructions on the packet. Drain well.

Melt the butter in a saucepan set over a low to medium heat and cook the onion and garlic, stirring occasionally, for 8–10 minutes, or until tender. Reduce the heat and stir in the flour. Cook for 1 minute until it thickens to a paste and then gradually add the milk, stirring and whisking until smooth and lump-free. Turn up the heat to medium and cook, stirring occasionally, until the sauce thickens to a coating consistency. Stir in the mustard, pumpkin spice mix, parsley and most of the cheese. Season to taste with salt and pepper.

Gently stir the cooked macaroni and roasted pumpkin into the sauce and transfer to a large buttered ovenproof baking dish. Sprinkle the chilli flakes and remaining cheese over the top.

Bake in the oven for 20–25 minutes, or until bubbling, crisp and golden brown. Add the breadcrumbs, drizzling them with a little oil, 10 minutes before the end. Serve immediately.

Variations

- Cook a sliced leek or some mushrooms with the onion.
- Mash the roasted pumpkin cubes before adding to the white sauce.
- Add some wilted fresh spinach to the sauce.
- Sprinkle with some chopped pancetta or Parma ham before covering with grated cheese.

DESSERTS

TRADITIONAL PUMPKIN PIE

///

No Thanksgiving celebration would be complete without a pumpkin pie. This one is so good that you can enjoy it all year round. If you are pressed for time, you can cheat and use a shop-bought pie shell.

SERVES 8
PREP 30 MINUTES
CHILL 30 MINUTES
COOK 1 HOUR

butter, for greasing
150g (5oz/¾ cup) soft light
  brown sugar
2 large free-range eggs plus
  1 egg yolk
2 tsp Pumpkin Spice Mix
  (see page 15), plus extra
  for dusting
450g (1lb/2 cups) Pumpkin
  Purée (see page 21)
240ml (8fl oz/1 cup) evaporated
  milk

**SHORTCRUST PASTRY
(PIE CRUST)**
200g (7oz/2 cups) plain
  (all-purpose) flour
a pinch of sea salt
100g (3½oz/scant ½ cup)
  chilled butter, diced
2–3 tbsp cold water

Make the pastry: sift the flour and salt into a mixing bowl. Rub in the butter with your fingertips until the mixture resembles breadcrumbs. Stir in enough cold water with a palette knife for the mixture to come together and form a dough. Use your hands to mould it into a ball, then wrap in cling film (plastic wrap) and chill in the fridge for at least 30 minutes.

Preheat the oven to 200°C (180°C fan)/400°F/gas 6. Lightly butter a 23cm (9 inch) tart tin (pan). Line a baking tray with baking parchment or kitchen foil.

Roll out the pastry on a lightly floured surface and use to line the tart tin, pressing it into the fluted sides. Level the top, cutting off any overhanging pastry. Place a sheet of baking parchment inside and fill with baking beans. Bake 'blind' in the oven for 15 minutes and then remove the paper and beans. Return to the oven for a further 5 minutes, or until the base is turning golden brown.

Remove the pastry case and reduce the oven temperature to 180°C (160°C fan)/350°F/gas 4.

Beat the sugar, eggs and yolk together in a large mixing bowl. Stir in the pumpkin spice mix, pumpkin purée and evaporated milk.

Pour into the pastry case and bake for 40–45 minutes, or until the filling sets. Don't worry if it's still a little wobbly – it will firm up as it cools down. Leave to cool in the tin on a wire rack for 1–2 hours.

Cut the pie into slices and serve with whipped cream or ice cream and a dusting of extra pumpkin spice mix. It will keep well in the fridge, covered, for 24 hours.

Variations

- Use double (heavy) cream instead of evaporated milk.
- Add some grated lemon or orange zest to the filling.
- Add 2–3 tablespoons cognac or dark rum.

PUMPKIN SPICED MERINGUES

//

Nothing beats homemade meringues – they taste so much better than bought ones and they're very easy to make. Although you can beat them by hand, it's quicker and easier to use a stand food mixer or a hand-held electric whisk.

MAKES 12 MERINGUES
PREP 15 MINUTES
COOK 2 HOURS

4 free-range egg whites
a pinch of salt
225g (8oz/1 cup) caster (superfine) sugar
½ tsp Pumpkin Spice Mix (see page 15)
Pumpkin Spice Whipped Cream (see page 17)

Tips: Store the meringues in an airtight container in a cool, dry place for up to 3 days. Fill with whipped cream just before serving.

For a more visually attractive effect, you can pipe the meringues in swirling circular shapes onto the lined baking trays before cooking.

Preheat the oven to 110°C (90°C fan)/225°F/gas ¼. Line two baking trays with baking parchment.

Using a stand food mixer or a hand-held electric whisk, beat the egg whites and salt until they form stiff peaks. Add 3 tablespoons of the sugar and beat until stiff and glossy. Fold in the rest of the sugar and the pumpkin spice mix in a figure-of-eight motion with a metal spoon.

Using a dessertspoon, drop spoonfuls of the mixture onto the lined baking trays, leaving plenty of space around them. You should end up with 12 meringues.

Bake for 2 hours, or until the meringues are dry. Peel them off the paper and leave on a wire rack until completely cold.

Sandwich the meringues together in pairs with the pumpkin spice whipped cream. Serve immediately.

Variations
- Add the seeds of a vanilla pod (bean) to the meringue mixture.
- Serve dusted with cinnamon or pumpkin spice mix.
- Add some grated or chopped chocolate to the whipped cream.
- Sandwich the meringues together with whipped cream flavoured with grated orange zest and diced stem ginger.

PUMPKIN SPICE TIRAMISU

///

Everyone loves tiramisu and the good news is that it's quick and easy to prep yourself at home, making it the perfect dessert for entertaining. Adding pumpkin spice and purée makes the mascarpone layer richer and creamier.

SERVES 4
PREP 15 MINUTES
CHILL 2–3 HOURS

1 egg yolk
2 tbsp vanilla sugar (see note)
1 tsp Pumpkin Spice Mix
    (see page 15)
250g (9oz/generous 1 cup)
    mascarpone
115g (4oz/½ cup) Pumpkin Purée
    (see page 21)
300ml (½ pint/1¼ cups) cooled
    espresso or strong black coffee
2 tbsp hazelnut or coffee liqueur
24 Savoiardi sponge fingers
    (ladyfinger cookies)
2 tbsp unsweetened cocoa
    powder

Variations
• Top with dark
  chocolate shavings.
• Substitute rum
  or Marsala for the
  liqueur.

Beat the egg yolk, sugar and pumpkin spice mix in a bowl until pale and creamy. Fold in the mascarpone until well combined and creamy, and then stir in the pumpkin purée.

Put the coffee and liqueur in a bowl and start dipping the sponge fingers (four to six at a time, depending on the size of your dish) into the mixture, allowing any excess to drop off. Dip for about 12 seconds – just long enough for them to absorb the liquid without falling apart.

Line the base of a glass serving dish with a layer of sponge fingers and cover with a layer of creamy mascarpone. Continue layering in this way until everything is used up, finishing with a layer of mascarpone.

Dust the top of the tiramisu with cocoa powder, then chill in the fridge for 2–3 hours until set.

Note: You can buy vanilla sugar or make it yourself by filling a glass jar with granulated or caster (superfine) sugar and placing a vanilla pod (bean) in it. Screw on the lid tightly and leave the vanilla to infuse the sugar with its flavour. As the level goes down, just top up with more beans and sugar.

SPICED BAKED APPLES

//

Sweet-and-spicy baked apples in their skins are probably the easiest dessert of all to make and the ultimate comfort food. If you have an apple tree in your garden, this is the perfect way to use up windfalls.

SERVES 4
PREP 15 MINUTES
COOK 50–55 MINUTES

4 large cooking apples (green apples), e.g. Bramley
2 tbsp water
50g (2oz/¼ cup) soft light brown sugar
1 tsp Pumpkin Spice Mix (see page 15)
30g (1oz/¼ cup) chopped walnuts
4 tbsp raisins or dried cranberries
4 tbsp butter, plus extra for dotting
4 tbsp clear honey, for drizzling

Preheat the oven to 180°C (160°C fan)/350°F/gas 4.

Use an apple corer to remove the cores and scoop out any seeds left inside the apples. Run a sharp knife around the circumference of each apple, just through the skin, so the apple flesh can expand when it is baked.

Stand the apples in an ovenproof baking dish and add the water.

In a bowl, mix the sugar, pumpkin spice mix, nuts and dried fruit together until combined.

Push a tablespoon of butter into the hollowed out centre of each apple and then fill with the dried fruit mixture. Dot the top with some more butter.

Bake, basting the apples once or twice with the cooking juices while they are cooking, for 45 minutes, or until tender, light and fluffy and the top half of the skin has separated from the bottom half. Drizzle with honey and pop back into the oven for 5–10 minutes.

Serve hot with some custard, pouring cream or ice cream.

Variations
· Drizzle with maple syrup instead of honey.
· Use dried cherries, apricots, dates or sultanas (seedless golden raisins) in the stuffing.
· Fill the apples with mincemeat or sugared blackberries.

Tip: If you want a really smooth panna cotta without any stringy pieces of pumpkin, strain the mixture through a muslin (cheesecloth)-lined sieve before pouring into the ramekins.

PUMPKIN SPICE PANNA COTTA

///

In Italian, *panna cotta* literally means 'cooked cream'. These quivering little creamy desserts are perfect for a Halloween or Thanksgiving dinner.

SERVES 6
PREP 20 MINUTES
COOK 10 MINUTES
CHILL 3+ HOURS

1 vanilla pod (bean)
2 tbsp cold water
3 tsp powdered gelatine
420ml (14fl oz/1¾ cups) double (heavy) cream
180ml (6fl oz/¾ cup) milk
50g (2oz/¼ cup) caster (superfine) sugar
115g (4oz/½ cup) Pumpkin Purée (see page 21)
1 tsp Pumpkin Spice Mix (see page 15)
salted caramel sauce, for drizzling

Variations
- Instead of a vanilla pod use a few drops of vanilla extract.
- Serve with a compôte of apples, pears, quinces or plums.

With a sharp knife, open the vanilla pod from end to end and scrape out the seeds. Set aside.

Put the cold water in a saucepan and sprinkle the gelatine over the top. Leave for 5 minutes until spongy and then set over a low heat for 5 minutes, stirring occasionally until the gelatine dissolves. Do not allow it to boil.

Place the vanilla pod and seeds in a saucepan with the cream, milk, sugar, pumpkin purée and pumpkin spice mix. Set over a low heat and cook gently for 5 minutes, stirring occasionally, until the sugar dissolves.

Remove the vanilla pod (don't discard it, see note on page 60) and stir in the dissolved gelatine.

Divide the mixture into six dariole moulds (molds) or 6cm (2½ inch) ramekins, then cover and chill in the fridge for at least 3 hours, or until the panna cotta sets. Don't worry if it's not super firm – it should be a soft set with the slightest hint of a wobble.

Unmould the panna cotta onto six serving plates. Carefully run a thin knife around the edge of the ramekins or moulds and invert them onto the plates. If the panna cotta doesn't drop out, quickly dip the base of the moulds or ramekins in a bowl of hot water and try again. Serve immediately, drizzled with salted caramel sauce.

PUMPKIN SPICE CRÈME BRÛLÉES

//

This is one of the easiest desserts ever to make and all you need are four ingredients. Using single (light) cream instead of double (heavy) whipping cream makes the crème brûlées less rich and cloying. They are the perfect way to round off a special meal.

SERVES 6
PREP 15 MINUTES
COOK 45–60 MINUTES
CHILL 3–5 HOURS

butter, for greasing
6 egg yolks
115g (4oz/½ cup) caster
   (superfine) sugar, plus extra
   for the caramel topping
1 tsp Pumpkin Spice Mix
   (see page 15)
600ml (1 pint/2½ cups) single
   (light) cream

Variations
· Mix a little ground
  cinnamon into the
  caster sugar before
  caramelizing.
· Sprinkle with
  demerara sugar
  instead of caster.

Preheat the oven to 150°C (130°C fan)/300°F/gas 2. Lightly butter six individual small ramekins.

Beat the egg yolks, sugar and pumpkin spice mix together in a bowl until well combined.

Heat the cream in a saucepan over a medium to high heat until it is almost boiling. Remove from the heat immediately and pour into the egg yolk and sugar mixture. Stir until combined, then strain through a sieve into a jug.

Place the ramekins in a large baking tin (pan) and pour cold water into the tray around them – enough to come halfway up their sides. Carefully pour the custard mixture into the ramekins.

Bake for 45–60 minutes, or until the custard is set and just firm to the touch. Remove and set aside to cool, then chill in the fridge for 3 hours.

Sprinkle a little sugar over each custard – just enough to cover the top – and caramelize with a cook's blow torch. If you don't have one, preheat an overhead grill (broiler) until it is really hot and place the ramekins in a grill pan underneath until the sugar turns to a golden brown caramel. Watch them carefully though as they can burn very quickly and easily.

Serve immediately or chill in the fridge for 2 hours before eating.

SPICY APPLE CRUMBLE

//

Apple crumble has to be the ultimate comfort food and maybe the easiest hot pudding to make. Ground cinnamon is often added to the apples and/or the crumble topping but this delicious recipe uses pumpkin spice mix instead, and the result is warmer and more rounded.

SERVES 4–6
PREP 15 MINUTES
COOK 30–40 MINUTES

1 tsp butter, for greasing
900g (2lb) cooking apples
(green apples), peeled, cored
and quartered
50g (2oz/¼ cup) dark or light
muscovado sugar
½ tsp Pumpkin Spice Mix
(see page 15)
juice of ½ lemon

CRUMBLE

200g (7oz/2 cups) plain
(all-purpose) flour
150g (5oz/¾ cup) chilled
unsalted butter, diced
50g (2oz/⅓ cup) ground almonds
(almond flour)
1 tsp Pumpkin Spice Mix
(see page 15)
115g (4oz/½ cup) golden caster
(superfine) sugar
a pinch of salt

Preheat the oven to 190°C (170°C fan)/375°F/gas 5. Butter a large shallow baking dish.

Make the crumble: put the flour and butter in a large bowl and rub in the butter with your fingertips until the mixture resembles breadcrumbs. Stir in the ground almonds, pumpkin spice mix, sugar and a pinch of salt. Drizzle with a little cold water and stir gently until some of the crumbs stick together.

Put the apples in the baking dish and toss them gently in the sugar and pumpkin spice mix. Sprinkle with lemon juice. Spoon the crumble topping over the top to completely cover the fruit.

Bake for 30–40 minutes or until golden brown and crisp on top with the juices starting to bubble through the crumble.

Serve warm with cream, custard, crème fraîche or ice cream.

Variations
· Add some chopped almonds or hazelnuts to the crumble.
· Stir in 2–3 tablespoons rolled or porridge oats.
· Add some blackberries with the apples.
· Instead of lemon juice, use some Calvados.

SPICED APPLE DUTCH BABY

///

Adding pumpkin and pumpkin spice to a Dutch baby gives it a delicious autumnal flavour. It's so simple to make and you can serve it as a dessert or even for breakfast or brunch.

SERVES 3–4
PREP 15 MINUTES
COOK 15–20 MINUTES

4 large free-range eggs
120ml (4fl oz/½ cup) milk
50g (2oz/¼ cup) Pumpkin Purée
  (see page 21)
1 tsp vanilla extract
50g (2oz/½ cup) plain
  (all-purpose) flour
3 tbsp white sugar
½ tsp Pumpkin Spice Mix
  (see page 15)
a good pinch of salt
2 tbsp unsalted butter
icing (confectioner's) sugar,
  for dusting

SPICY APPLE FILLING

50g (2oz/¼ cup) unsalted butter
50g (2oz/¼ cup) light muscovado
  sugar
3 large dessert (sweet) apples,
  peeled, cored and thickly
  sliced
a pinch of Pumpkin Spice Mix
  (see page 15)

Preheat the oven to 230°C (210°C fan)/450°F/gas 8. Put in a 23cm (9 inch) cast-iron or oven-safe frying pan (skillet) and leave to heat.

Whisk the eggs, milk, pumpkin purée, vanilla extract, flour, sugar, pumpkin spice mix and salt in a bowl or blitz in a blender or food processor until you have a smooth batter.

Add the butter to the hot frying pan and swirl it around to coat the base and sides. Quickly pour in the batter and bake for 15–20 minutes, or until set, puffed and golden.

Meanwhile, make the spicy apple filling: melt the butter in a frying pan set over a medium to high heat. Stir in the sugar and add the apple and pumpkin spice mix. Cook, stirring occasionally, for 10 minutes, or until the apples are tender and just starting to caramelize.

Slide the pancake out of the pan onto a serving plate and fill with the apples. Dust with icing sugar, then cut into slices and serve immediately while it's piping hot with cream or ice cream.

Variations
· Use pears, quinces, greengages or plums instead of apples.
· Substitute non-dairy almond or oat milk for regular milk.
· Sprinkle with vanilla sugar (see page 60).

SPICED APPLE PIE

//

Nothing says real home cooking like a crisp apple pie filled with juicy fruit. The pumpkin spice enhances the flavour and turns it into something really special.

SERVES 6
PREP 20 MINUTES
CHILL 30 MINUTES
COOK 50 MINUTES

900g (2lb) cooking apples
    (green apples), e.g. Bramley,
    peeled, cored and quartered
150g (5oz/generous ½ cup)
    caster (superfine) sugar
1 tsp Pumpkin Spice Mix (page 15)
juice of 1 lemon
1 tbsp chilled butter, diced
1 egg white

SHORTCRUST PASTRY (PIE CRUST)

350g (12oz/3½ cups) plain
    (all-purpose) flour
a pinch of salt
175g (6oz/¾ cup) chilled butter,
    diced, plus extra for greasing
2–3 tbsp cold water

Variations
• Use brown sugar
  with the apples for a
  caramel flavour.

Make the shortcrust pastry: sift the flour and salt into a mixing bowl. Rub in the butter with your fingertips until the mixture resembles breadcrumbs. Stir in enough cold water with a palette knife for the mixture to come together and form a dough. Use your hands to mould it into a ball, then wrap in cling film (plastic wrap) and chill in the fridge for at least 30 minutes.

Preheat the oven to 190°C (170°C fan)/375°F/gas 5. Place a baking tray in the oven to heat up. Lightly butter a 20cm (8 inch) loose-bottomed tart tin (pan).

Roll out about two-thirds of the pastry on a lightly floured surface and use to line the tart tin, pressing it into the fluted sides. Don't worry about any overhanging pastry.

In a bowl, toss the apples in 125g (4½oz/generous ½ cup) of the sugar and the pumpkin spice mix. Transfer to the pastry case and sprinkle with the lemon juice and diced butter.

Roll out the remaining pastry and cut into a circle large enough to cover the top of the pie. Fold the overhanging pastry from the base over the edge and press together to seal. Brush the top with egg white and sprinkle with the remaining sugar. If wished, decorate the edge by pressing down lightly with a fork. Make two small incisions in the top to allow the steam to escape.

Place the pie on the hot baking tray and bake for 20 minutes and then reduce the temperature to 170°C (150°C fan)/325°F/gas 3 for 30 minutes, or until the pastry is golden. Serve hot or cold with custard, cream or ice cream.

SPICED BREAD-AND-BUTTER PUDDING

///

Traditionally, bread puddings were a way of using up leftover bread, so nothing went to waste.
It may be economical and frugal but a creamy bread-and-butter pudding is one of the most
delicious desserts you can eat – comfort food at its best.

SERVES 4-6
PREP 15 MINUTES
STAND 10-15 MINUTES
COOK 40-45 MINUTES

6 medium-cut slices of
    white bread
2 tbsp butter, plus extra for
    greasing
115g (4oz) dried fruit, e.g. raisins,
    currants, sultanas (golden
    raisins)
3 free-range eggs
50g (2oz/¼ cup) caster
    (superfine) sugar
240ml (8fl oz/1 cup) full-fat milk
200ml (7fl oz/scant 1 cup) single
    (light) cream
1 tsp vanilla extract
1 tsp Pumpkin Spice Mix
    (see page 15)
2 tbsp vanilla sugar (see page 60)

Preheat the oven to 180°C (160°C fan)/350°F/gas 4.
Generously butter a 1-litre (34fl oz) baking dish.

Cut each slice of bread in half diagonally and spread with butter.
Place them, overlapping each other, in the dish. Sprinkle all over
with the dried fruit.

In a bowl, beat the eggs and sugar until well combined.

Heat the milk and cream in a saucepan set over a medium to
high heat. Just before it boils, remove from the heat and stir into
the egg mixture with the vanilla extract and pumpkin spice. Pour
the custard over the bread and dried fruit and set aside for about
10–15 minutes to soak.

Sprinkle the vanilla sugar over the top and stand the dish in a
roasting tin (pan). Pour enough cold water into the pan to come
halfway up the sides of the dish and bake for 40–45 minutes, or
until the custard is set and wobbly and golden brown on top.

Serve hot on its own or with cream and some stewed or puréed
seasonal fruit.

Variations
· Substitute dried cranberries for the raisins, currants
  and sultanas.
· Gently drizzle some warmed apricot jam over the
  cooked pudding and dust with icing (confectioner's) sugar.

EASY-PEASY CRUNCHY GINGER TRIFLE

//

The beauty of this no-bake trifle is that it's so quick and easy to make. It uses store cupboard and supermarket ingredients and is perfect for throwing together at the last minute for unexpected guests. If you want a very boozy trifle, add more Cointreau.

SERVES 4–6
PREP 20 MINUTES
CHILL 45 MINUTES+

225g (8oz) gingernuts or crisp ginger biscuits (cookies)
300g (10oz/generous 1 cup) diced mango
6 knobs of stem ginger in syrup, drained
4 tbsp Cointreau
2 tsp Pumpkin Spice Mix (page 15)
500ml (17fl oz/generous 2 cups) fresh vanilla custard
300ml (½ pint/1¼ cups) whipping cream
2 tbsp ginger syrup (from the stem ginger jar)
grated zest of 1 orange
dark (bittersweeet) chocolate shavings, for sprinkling

Tip: Do not crush the gingernuts to crumbs. You need to end up with crisp, large-ish pieces, so they stay slightly crunchy.

Break the gingernuts into chunks (quarters or a little smaller) with your fingers. Transfer them to a glass trifle/dessert bowl and sprinkle the mango and stem ginger over the top.

Sprinkle the Cointreau over and chill for 15 minutes to allow the gingernuts to absorb the flavour.

Stir the pumpkin spice mix into the custard and pour over the fruity gingernut mixture. Chill in the fridge for at least 30 minutes to allow the custard to firm up.

Beat the cream and ginger syrup in a stand food mixer or with a hand-held electric whisk until it stands in soft peaks. Gently stir in the orange zest and then spoon or pipe over the top of the trifle.

Chill in the fridge until required or serve immediately, sprinkled with chocolate shavings. The trifle will keep well in the fridge for 2 days before the gingernuts lose their crunch.

Variations
- Decorate with crystallized ginger or fresh pomegranate seeds.
- Instead of mango use diced juicy pear or mandarin segments.
- Use Grand Marnier or brandy instead of Cointreau.
- Line the bowl with sliced shop-bought ginger cake soaked in brandy or Marsala before adding the gingernut pieces.

BAKING

PUMPKIN SCONES

//

These yummy scones freeze well for up to 2 months and can be defrosted at room temperature and then reheated in a hot oven for 10 minutes.

MAKES 8–10 SCONES
PREP 20 MINUTES
COOK 12–15 MINUTES

200g (7oz/2 cups) plain
  (all-purpose) flour, plus
  extra for dusting
2 tsp baking powder
½ tsp bicarbonate of soda
  (baking soda)
½ tsp sea salt
2 tsp Pumpkin Spice Mix (page 15)
50g (2oz/¼ cup) soft light
  brown sugar
115g (4oz/½ cup) chilled
  butter, diced
1 large free-range egg
60ml (2fl oz/¼ cup) double
  (heavy) cream
2 tsp vanilla extract
115g (4oz/½ cup) Pumpkin
  Purée (see page 21)
beaten egg, to glaze

Preheat the oven to 200°C (180°C fan)/400°F/gas 6. Line a baking tray with baking parchment.

Using a food processor (see note below), process the flour, baking powder, bicarbonate of soda, sea salt, pumpkin spice mix and sugar until well combined. Add the butter and pulse until the mixture is crumbly and resembles breadcrumbs.

In a bowl, whisk the egg with the cream and vanilla extract. Beat in the pumpkin purée and add to the food processor. Pulse until you have a slightly sticky dough.

Place on a lightly floured work surface and knead with your hands until the dough comes together and is smooth. Roll out to a thickness of 2.5cm (1 inch) and cut into rounds with a fluted 5cm (2 inch) round cutter. Use up any leftover dough and trimmings by re-rolling them and cutting out more scones.

Place the scones on the lined baking tray and brush the tops with beaten egg. Bake for 12–15 minutes until well risen and golden brown.

Transfer to a wire rack to cool and serve warm or cold, plain or split and buttered. The scones will keep well in an airtight container for 2–3 days and, if wished, can be warmed before eating.

Variations
- Add some ground ginger to the mix.
- Add some sultanas (golden raisins).

Note: If you don't have a food processor, put all the dry ingredients in a large bowl, mix well and then rub in the diced butter with your fingertips. Add the liquid ingredients and stir until you have a slightly sticky dough.

PUMPKIN SPICE SHORTBREAD

//

This rich and buttery shortbread is enhanced with the addition of pumpkin spice. It's the perfect companion for a mid-afternoon or teatime cup of tea. Don't leave out the rice flour – it's what gives the shortbread its distinctive crunch and melt-in-the-mouth texture.

MAKES 16 SQUARES
PREP 15 MINUTES
COOK 20–25 MINUTES

200g (7oz/2 cups) plain
   (all-purpose) flour
100g (3½oz/⅔ cup) rice flour
1 tsp Pumpkin Spice Mix
   (see page 15)
100g (3½oz/scant ½ cup) caster
   (superfine) sugar
200g (7oz/scant 1 cup) butter,
   diced, plus extra for greasing

PUMPKIN SPICE SUGAR
50g (2oz/¼ cup) caster
   (superfine) sugar
1 tsp Pumpkin Spice Mix
   (see page 15)

Tip: If wished, blitz the butter and sugar in a food processor, then add the flours and spice mix. Pulse until the mixture resembles breadcrumbs.

Preheat the oven to 180°C (160°C fan)/350°F/gas 4. Lightly butter a 20cm (8 inch) square cake tin (baking pan).

Mix the flour, rice flour, pumpkin spice mix and sugar in a large bowl. Add the butter and rub together until it resembles fine breadcrumbs. Lightly bring the mixture together with your hands to form a soft dough. Transfer to a bowl or work surface and work with your hands into a ball of dough.

Transfer to the buttered cake tin and press the mixture down firmly, levelling the top. Prick several times with a fork and then bake for 20–25 minutes or until pale golden.

Meanwhile, make the pumpkin spice sugar: mix the sugar and pumpkin spice in a bowl.

While the shortbread is still warm but has firmed up a little, cut into squares or wedges and dredge with the pumpkin spice sugar. Set aside until cold. The shortbreads will keep well in an airtight container for up to 1 week.

Variations
- Cover with melted dark (bittersweet) chocolate and leave to set before cutting into squares.
- Substitute ground cinnamon for the pumpkin spice.
- Use cornflour (cornstarch) instead of rice flour.

SPICY FLAPJACKS

//

These yummy flapjacks, infused with pumpkin spice, are deliciously sweet, nutty and crunchy. They are packed with low-GI oats, dried fruit and nuts, making them high in fibre and full of nutritional goodness.

MAKES 9 FLAPJACKS
PREP 15 MINUTES
COOK 20–25 MINUTES

175g (6oz/¾ cup) unsalted butter, plus extra for greasing
1 tbsp golden syrup (corn syrup)
100g (3½oz/½ cup) soft light brown sugar
grated zest of 1 orange
250g (9oz/3 cups) jumbo rolled oats
2 tsp Pumpkin Spice Mix (see page 15)
a pinch of sea salt
85g (3oz/scant ¾ cup) dried cranberries
50g (2oz/scant ½ cup) chopped nuts, e.g. pistachios, pecans, walnuts
50g (2oz/⅓ cup) white chocolate chips

Preheat the oven to 170°C (150°C fan)/325°F/gas 3. Butter a 20cm (8 inch) square cake tin (baking pan) and line with baking parchment.

Melt the butter in a saucepan set over a low heat. Add the golden syrup and sugar and stir gently until the sugar dissolves.

Remove the pan from the heat and add the orange zest, oats, pumpkin spice mix, sea salt, cranberries and nuts.

Transfer to the lined tin, pressing the mixture into the corners. Push the white chocolate chips into the top and then level it with a palette knife until smooth. Bake for 20–25 minutes until golden brown.

Remove from the oven and set aside to cool. After 10 minutes, cut into nine squares and leave until the flapjacks are completely cold. They will keep well stored in an airtight container for up to 5 days.

Variations
· Cover the flapjacks with melted chocolate.
· Use raisins, sultanas, dried cherries or apricots.
· Add some chopped candied orange peel.
· Substitute dark (bittersweet) chocolate for white.

PUMPKIN SPICED GINGER CAKE

//

Adding pumpkin spice mix to a traditional ginger cake makes it taste deliciously spicy and adds depth of flavour. To enjoy it at its best, leave it for a day before cutting and eating – the flavours will intensify.

SERVES 8
PREP 20 MINUTES
COOK 50 MINUTES

115g (4oz/scant ½ cup) golden syrup (corn syrup)
60g (2oz/¼ cup) butter, plus extra for greasing
100g (3½oz/1 cup) plain (all-purpose) flour
30g (1oz/¼ cup) self-raising (self-rising) flour
1 tsp bicarbonate of soda (baking soda)
a pinch of sea salt
2 tsp Pumpkin Spice Mix (see page 15)
100g (3½oz/½ cup) dark muscovado sugar
120ml (4fl oz/½ cup) milk
1 free-range egg
grated zest and juice of 1 orange
4 knobs of stem ginger in syrup, chopped, plus extra for decoration

LEMON ICING
115g (4oz/1 cup) icing (confectioner's) sugar
2 tbsp lemon juice

Preheat the oven to 170°C (150°C fan)/325°F/gas 3. Butter a 900g (2lb) loaf tin (pan) and line the base with baking parchment.

Stir the golden syrup and butter together in a saucepan set over a low heat until the butter melts.

Sift the flours and bicarbonate of soda into a large bowl. Stir in the salt, pumpkin spice mix and sugar.

Beat the milk and egg together and stir into the flour mixture, mixing well. Stir in the orange zest and juice and then add the melted butter and syrup, a little at a time, mixing between each addition. Stir in the stem ginger.

Transfer to the lined loaf tin and bake for 50 minutes, or until the cake is well risen and a skewer inserted into the centre comes out clean. Remove from the oven and leave in the tin for 10 minutes before turning out onto a wire rack.

Make the lemon icing: sift the icing sugar into a bowl and gradually stir in enough lemon juice to make a smooth icing.

When the cake is cold, cover with the lemon icing and decorate the top with some chopped stem ginger. Leave to set and cut into slices to serve. It stays moist and fresh for 4–5 days if wrapped in kitchen foil.

Variations
- Replace some of the golden syrup with black treacle.
- Add some diced or grated fresh root ginger to the cake mixture.
- Add a little Pumpkin Purée (see page 21) and raisins.
- For a more gingery flavour, add a little stem ginger syrup.

EASY-PEASY CHEESECAKE

//

This speedy cheesecake is a bit of a cheat but it's perfect when you're in a hurry and don't have time to make a more traditional dessert. What's more, even though it doesn't require any cooking or specialist skills, it tastes fabulous.

SERVES 6–8
PREP 20 MINUTES
CHILL 1 HOUR

250g (9oz) gingernuts or crisp ginger biscuits (cookies)
115g (4oz/½ cup) butter
1 tsp Pumpkin Spice Mix (see page 15)
250g (9oz/generous 1 cup) mascarpone
175g (6oz/generous ½ cup) lemon curd
2 knobs of stem ginger in syrup, diced

TOPPING
300ml (½ pint/1¼ cups) whipping cream
Pumpkin Spice Mix (see page 15), for dusting
3 tbsp chopped walnuts or pecans
caramel sauce, for drizzling

Put the biscuits in a food processor and blitz to crumbs. Alternatively, put them in a sealed zip-lock bag and bash with a rolling pin to crush.

Melt the butter in a saucepan set over a low to medium heat and stir in the biscuit crumbs and pumpkin spice mix. Tip the mixture into a loose-bottomed 23cm (9 inch) tart tin (pan) and press down firmly and evenly with the back of a spoon to line the base and sides. Chill in the fridge for 1 hour, or until set firm.

Put the mascarpone in a bowl and swirl in the lemon curd and stem ginger together with a little syrup. Use to fill the tart case, spreading the filling out to the sides and levelling the top. At this stage, you can place the cheesecake in the fridge until you're ready to serve it.

Just before serving, whip the cream until it stands in soft peaks and spoon over the cheesecake or pipe around the edges, depending on how informal you want it to look. Dust with the pumpkin spice mix and sprinkle the nuts oer the cream, then drizzle with caramel sauce.

Variations
· Drizzle with chocolate sauce, Pumpkin Spice Syrup (see page 18) or maple syrup.
· If you're in a rush, top with fresh strawberries or raspberries and omit the cream.

CHURROS

//

Churros are Spanish 'doughnuts' and are usually eaten warm and freshly fried for breakfast, often with chocolate sauce. We've dredged ours with pumpkin-spiced sugar to make them extra special.

SERVES 6
PREP 15 MINUTES
COOK 12–15 MINUTES

50g (2oz/¼ cup) butter
240ml (8fl oz/1 cup) water
a good pinch of sea salt
100g (3½oz/1 cup) plain
   (all-purpose) flour
1 large free-range egg, beaten
vegetable or sunflower oil, for
   deep-frying
chocolate sauce, for drizzling or
   dipping (optional)

PUMPKIN SPICE SUGAR
100g (3½oz/scant ½ cup) caster
   (superfine) sugar
1 tsp Pumpkin Spice Mix
   (see page 15)

Tip: If you don't have a sugar thermometer, drop a small bread cube into the hot oil. It's ready if the bread turns golden brown in 30 seconds.

Put the butter, water and salt in a pan set over a medium to high heat and bring to the boil. Tip in the flour and cook, beating all the time, until you have a smooth dough that forms a ball and comes away from the sides of the pan.

Remove the pan from the heat and beat in the egg, a little at a time.

Heat the oil in a deep, heavy-based saucepan or a deep-fat fryer to 180°C (350°F) – use a sugar thermometer to measure this.

Meanwhile, put the churro dough in a piping (pastry) bag fitted with a 1cm (½ inch) star nozzle (tip) and pipe into 12cm (5 inch) strips.

Fry the strips in batches, being careful not to overload the pan, for 3–4 minutes, or until golden brown and crisp. Remove with a slotted spoon and drain on kitchen paper (paper towels).

Mix the sugar and pumpkin spice mix together and use to dredge the piping hot churros. Serve immediately with chocolate sauce (if using) for drizzling or dipping.

Variations
- Serve with salted caramel sauce or dulce de leche.
- Add ½ teaspoon vanilla extract with the egg.

SPICY APPLE CRUMBLE CAKE

//

This warmly spiced cake is deliciously fruity and moist with a crunchy crumble topping. It's perfect for serving as a treat, at teatime or as a dessert with cream, crème fraîche, yoghurt, ice cream or custard.

SERVES 9
PREP 25 MINUTES
COOK 50–60 MINUTES

450g (1lb) cooking apples
    (green apples), e.g. Bramley,
    peeled, cored and cubed
juice of 1 lemon
2 tbsp water
175g (6oz/¾ cup) caster
    (superfine) sugar, plus 4 tbsp
175g (6oz/¾ cup) softened
    butter, plus extra for greasing
2 large free-range eggs
175g (6oz/1¾ cups) self-raising
    (self-rising) flour, sifted
1 tsp Pumpkin Spice Mix
    (see page 15)
50g (2oz/⅓ cup) ground almonds
    (almond flour)

CRUMBLE TOPPING
50g (2oz/½ cup) plain
    (all-purpose) flour
1 tsp Pumpkin Spice Mix
    (see page 15)
50g (2oz/¼ cup) chilled
    butter, diced
2 tbsp demerara sugar

Preheat the oven to 160°C (140°C fan)/315°F/gas 3. Grease and line a 20cm (8 inch) square cake tin (baking pan) with baking parchment.

Make the crumble topping: put the flour and pumpkin spice mix in a bowl and rub in the butter with your fingertips until the mixture has the consistency of breadcrumbs. Stir in the sugar and set aside.

Put the apple, lemon juice, water and 4 tablespoons sugar in a saucepan and set over a low heat. Stir gently until the sugar dissolves and then increase the heat and bring to the boil. Turn the heat down as low as it will go and cook, covered, for 5 minutes, or until the apple is just tender. Set aside.

Using a stand food mixer or a hand-held electric whisk, beat the sugar and butter until pale and creamy. Beat in the eggs, one at a time, adding a spoonful of flour with each addition. Lightly beat in the flour, pumpkin spice mix and ground almonds.

Transfer to the lined cake tin and sprinkle the cooked apple over the top, pressing it down slightly into the cake mixture. Cover with the crumble topping and then bake for 50–60 minutes, or until golden brown and a skewer inserted into the centre comes out clean.

Leave in the tin to cool for about 30 minutes. Cut into squares to serve either warm or at room temperature. The cake will keep well for 2–3 days stored in an airtight container in the fridge.

Variations

- Add chopped hazelnuts or flaked almonds to the crumble mixture.
- Add some blackberries to the apples.
- Add some almond or vanilla extract to the cake mixture.

PUMPKIN SPICE CRANBERRY OAT MUFFINS

These delicious muffins are packed with nutritional goodness and are great for a quick snack, a packed lunch treat or even breakfast on-the-go. What's more, they're quick and easy to make and keep well.

MAKES 12 MUFFINS
PREP 15 MINUTES
COOK 20–25 MINUTES

100g (3½oz/1 cup) rolled oats
200g (7oz/2 cups) plain (all-purpose) flour
2 tsp baking powder
1 tsp bicarbonate of soda (baking soda)
¼ tsp sea salt
2 tsp Pumpkin Spice Mix (see page 15)
100g (3½oz/½ cup) soft light brown sugar
3 large ripe bananas
2 free-range eggs, beaten
85g (3oz/⅓ cup) butter, melted
240ml (8fl oz/1 cup) milk
150g (5oz/1½ cups) fresh cranberries (or frozen)
25g (1oz/¼ cup) rolled oats
25g (1oz/⅛ cup) demerara sugar

Tip: These freeze well for up to 3 months.

Preheat the oven to 180°C (160°C fan)/350°F/gas 4. Line a 12-hole muffin tin (pan) with paper cases (liners).

In a large bowl, mix together the oats, flour, baking powder, bicarbonate of soda, salt, pumpkin spice mix and sugar. Make a well in the centre.

In another bowl, mash the bananas with a fork and stir in the beaten eggs, melted butter and half of the milk.

Pour the mixture into the dry ingredients and mix together lightly – don't over-mix. Gently fold in the cranberries, distributing them throughout the mixture. If it seems a little dry, add the remaining milk.

Divide the mixture into the paper cases and sprinkle with the oats and demerara sugar. Bake for about 20–25 minutes, or until golden brown and a skewer inserted in the centre of a muffin comes out clean.

Leave to cool on a wire rack and eat slightly warm or at room temperature. The muffins will keep well for 4–5 days if stored in an airtight container in the fridge.

Variations
· Flavour with vanilla extract.
· Substitute blueberries for cranberries.
· Add some dark (bittersweet) chocolate chips.

CRUNCHY PUMPKIN MUFFINS

//

These crunchy-topped moist and spicy muffins are delicious to eat at any time of the year.

MAKES 12 MUFFINS
PREP 20 MINUTES
COOK 20 MINUTES

200g (7oz/2 cups) plain
    (all-purpose) flour
1 tsp baking powder
1 tsp bicarbonate of soda
    (baking soda)
2 tsp Pumpkin Spice Mix (page 15)
½ tsp sea salt
115g (4oz/½ cup) butter,
    at room temperature
150g (5oz/¾ cup) soft light
    brown sugar
2 free-range eggs
400g (14oz/1¾ cups) Pumpkin
    Purée (see page 21)
2 tbsp milk
2 knobs of stem ginger in
    syrup, diced
icing (confectioner's) sugar, to dust

STREUSEL TOPPING
45g (1½oz/scant ½ cup)
    plain (all-purpose) flour
½ tsp ground cinnamon
a pinch of sea salt
60g (2oz/¼ cup) demerara sugar
100g (3½oz) chopped walnuts
85g (3oz/⅓ cup) melted butter
1½ tsp ginger syrup (from the
    stem ginger jar)

Preheat the oven to 190°C (170°C fan)/375°F/gas 5. Fill a 12-hole muffin tin (pan) with paper cases (liners).

Sift the flour, baking powder, bicarbonate of soda, pumpkin pie spice and salt into a bowl and mix well.

In a large bowl, beat the butter and sugar until light and fluffy with a hand-held electric whisk. Beat in the eggs, one at a time, and then the pumpkin purée and milk. Stir in the stem ginger. Gently fold in the flour and spice mixture until well combined. Do not beat or over-mix. Divide the mixture into the paper cases.

Make the streusel topping: mix together the flour, cinnamon, salt, sugar and walnuts in a bowl. Stir in the melted butter and ginger syrup. Sprinkle over the muffins, pressing it lightly into the mixture.

Bake for 20 minutes, or until cooked, golden brown and crunchy on top. When a thin skewer is inserted into the centre, it should come out clean.

Leave the muffins to cool in the tin for 10 minutes and then transfer to a wire rack. When cold, lightly dust with icing sugar. Store in an airtight container in the fridge for up to 5 days.

Variations
- Use hazelnuts or almonds instead of walnuts.
- Instead of the streusel topping, sprinkle with roasted pumpkin seeds.
- Fold in some sultanas (golden raisins).
- Use melted coconut oil or vegetable oil instead of butter.

AUTUMN PLUM TRAYBAKE

///

This moist traybake-style cake made with autumnal fruit and seasoned with pumpkin spice mix makes a great seasonal treat. Serve it with some ice cream, crème fraîche or whipped cream.

SERVES 8–10
PREP 20 MINUTES
COOK 35–40 MINUTES

175 (6oz/¾ cup) butter,
   plus extra for greasing
175g (6oz/generous ¾ cup)
   soft light brown sugar
3 free-range eggs
85g (3oz/scant 1 cup) plain
   (all-purpose) flour
1 tsp baking powder
2 tsp Pumpkin Spice Mix
   (see page 15)
115g (4oz/¾ cup) ground
   almonds (almond flour)
grated zest and juice of 1 orange
seeds of 1 vanilla pod (bean)
2–3 tbsp milk
12 ripe plums, halved and
   stoned (pitted)
85g (3oz/generous ½ cup)
   whole hazelnuts
icing (confectioner's) sugar,
   for dusting

Preheat the oven to 180°C (160°C fan)/350°F/gas 4. Grease and line a shallow 30 x 20cm (12 x 8 inch) cake tin (baking pan) with baking parchment.

In a stand food mixer, beat the butter and sugar until soft and fluffy. Add the eggs, one at a time, beating well between each addition. Add a spoonful of flour with them, if wished, to prevent the mixture from curdling.

Sift in the flour, baking powder and pumpkin spice mix, then add the ground almonds. Mix on a slow speed until well combined. Add the orange zest and juice, vanilla seeds and enough milk to slacken the mixture.

Transfer to the prepared cake tin and level the top, pushing the mixture into the corners of the tin. Arrange the plums, cut-side up, in neat lines on top of the cake, then press them down slightly into the mixture. Press the hazelnuts into the cake around them.

Bake for about 35–40 minutes, or until the cake rises around the fruit and a skewer inserted into the centre comes out clean. Leave to cool in the tin and then lightly dust with icing sugar.

Serve the cake cut into squares or slices. If wrapped in kitchen foil, it will keep in the refrigerator for up to 3 days. Bring to room temperature before serving.

Variations
• Use pears, greengages or cherries instead of plums.

SPICY PUMPKIN CARROT CAKE

//

Adding pumpkin spice and pumpkin purée to a carrot cake makes it deliciously moist and warmly spiced. It's so good that you can enjoy it all year round.

SERVES 8–10
PREP 20 MINUTES
COOK 35–40 MINUTES

175g (6oz/generous ¾ cup)
   soft light brown sugar
85ml (3fl oz/generous ¼ cup)
   sunflower or coconut oil
3 free-range eggs, beaten
115g (4oz/½ cup) Pumpkin
   Purée (see page 21)
225g (8oz/3 cups) grated
   raw carrots
grated zest of 1 orange
175g (6oz/1¾ cups) self-raising
   (self-rising) flour
½ tsp baking powder
2 tsp Pumpkin Spice Mix
   (see page 15)
1 tsp ground cinnamon
milk, for slackening (optional)
chopped pistachios, for
   decoration

FROSTING
115g (4oz/½ cup) cream cheese
   (at room temperature)
50g (2oz/¼ cup) softened butter
grated zest of 1 orange
250g (9oz/2 cups) icing
   (confectioner's) sugar

Preheat the oven to 180°C (160°C fan)/350°F/gas 4. Line a 20cm (8 inch) square cake tin (baking pan) with baking parchment.

In a mixing bowl or food processor, beat together the sugar, oil and eggs until well blended.

Mix in the pumpkin purée, grated carrots and orange zest. Sift in the flour, baking powder and spices and mix thoroughly. If the mixture is too stiff, slacken it with a little milk.

Pour the mixture into the lined cake tin and bake for 40–45 minutes, or until well risen, golden brown and a skewer inserted into the centre comes out clean. Leave to cool on a wire rack.

Meanwhile, make the cream cheese frosting: using a stand food mixer or hand-held electric whisk, beat the cream cheese, butter and orange zest until well blended and smooth. On a low speed, gradually beat in the sugar, a little at a time. Continue beating on a high speed until the frosting is creamy and fluffy.

When the cake is cold, cover with the frosting and sprinkle with the chopped pistachios. Serve cut into squares or slices. The cake will keep well for up to 4 days stored in an airtight container.

Tip: Use butter and cream cheese at room temperature rather than straight from the fridge to make the frosting.

HALLOWEEN PUMPKIN SPICE CUPCAKES

///

These little cupcakes are simple to make, speedy to cook and easy to decorate. They are perfect for parties and trick-or-treating – children love the ghostly faces.

MAKES 12 CUPCAKES
PREP 30 MINUTES
COOK 12-15 MINUTES

150g (5oz/⅔ cup)
   softened butter
125g (4½oz/generous ½ cup)
   caster (superfine) sugar
2 free-range eggs
1 tsp vanilla extract
150g (5oz/1½ cups) self-raising
   (self-rising) flour
2 tsp Pumpkin Spice Mix
   (see page 15)
2 tbsp milk

FROSTING

115g (4oz/½ cup) cream cheese
   (at room temperature)
50g (2oz/¼ cup) softened butter
180g (6oz/1½ cups) icing
   (confectioner's) sugar
1 tsp vanilla extract
1 tsp Pumpkin Spice Mix
   (see page 15)
24 dark (bittersweet) chocolate
   chips, for decoration

Preheat the oven to 180°C (160°C fan)/350°F/gas 4. Line a 12-hole muffin tin (pan) with paper cases (liners).

In a stand food mixer or using a hand-held electric whisk, beat the butter and sugar until pale, light and fluffy. Beat in the eggs, one at a time, and then the vanilla.

Sift in the flour and pumpkin spice and mix in gently on a low setting. Add the milk and mix gently until smooth.

Divide into the paper cases and bake for 12–15 minutes, until well risen and golden. Leave in the tin for 5 minutes and then transfer the cupcakes to a wire rack and set aside until completely cold.

Make the frosting: using a hand-held electric whisk, beat together the cream cheese and butter until smooth. On a low speed, add the icing sugar, a little at a time, and keep beating until smooth and fluffy. Beat in the vanilla and pumpkin spice mix.

Fill a piping (pastry) bag fitted with a plain nozzle (tip) and pipe an upside-down cone shape on top of each cupcake to resemble a ghost. Add two chocolate chips near the top for 'eyes'. The cupcakes will keep for up to 3 days stored in an airtight container.

Variations
· Dust with cinnamon or extra pumpkin spice mix.
· Decorate with Smarties or liquorice allsorts to make funny faces.

SPIDERWEB PUMPKIN COOKIES

These moist cookies have a lovely sweet-and-spicy flavour and a slightly soft and chewy texture. Children will enjoy the marshmallow spiderweb topping.

MAKES 20 COOKIES
PREP 25 MINUTES
COOK 15–20 MINUTES

225g (8oz/2¼ cups) plain (all-purpose) flour
1 tsp baking powder
1 tsp bicarbonate of soda (baking soda)
2 tsp Pumpkin Spice Mix (see page 15)
½ tsp sea salt
125g (4½oz/generous ½ cup) softened butter
200g (7oz/1 cup) soft light brown sugar
115g (4oz/½ cup) Pumpkin Purée (see page 21)
1 free-range egg
1 tsp vanilla extract

SPIDERWEB
300g (10oz) marshmallows

Tips: The pumpkin purée should not be too liquid. Strain off any excess liquid or pat gently with paper towels to absorb it.

Preheat the oven to 180°C (160°C fan)/350°F/gas 4. Line two baking trays with baking parchment.

Put the flour, baking powder, bicarbonate of soda, pumpkin spice mix and salt in a large mixing bowl.

Using a stand food mixer or hand-held electric whisk, beat the butter and sugar until pale, light and fluffy. Beat in the pumpkin purée, egg and vanilla until well combined.

Tip the dry ingredients into the bowl and mix well until they combine and form a soft dough.

Take heaped tablespoons or cookie scoops of the dough and shape into balls. Place on the lined baking trays, leaving plenty of space around each one, and flatten them slightly but not too much. Bake for 15–20 minutes, or until just firm but still a little soft in the centre. Cool on a wire rack.

Make the spiderweb: put the marshmallows in a bowl and microwave for 1 minute. Stir and continue to microwave in 15-second bursts until melted. Allow to cool a little but not too much or it will harden up.

When it is cool enough to handle, take a little of the mixture and stretch it between your fingers. Cover the cooled cookies with the marshmallow strands to create a criss-cross spiderweb effect. The cookies will keep well stored in an airtight container for up to 4 days.

CRANBERRY PUMPKIN LOAF

///

This warmly spiced and fragrant pumpkin bread is studded with juicy cranberries and makes a lovely alternative to banana bread. Store in an airtight container for up to 3 days.

MAKES 2 LOAVES
PREP 20 MINUTES
COOK 55–60 MINUTES

225g (8oz/2¼ cups) plain (all-purpose) flour
1 tsp bicarbonate of soda (baking soda)
1 tsp baking powder
½ tsp sea salt
1 tbsp Pumpkin Spice Mix (see page 15)
175g (6oz/¾ cup) softened butter
200g (7oz/scant 1 cup) caster (superfine) sugar, plus extra for sprinkling
200g (7oz/1 cup) soft light brown sugar
2 large free-range eggs
400g (14oz/1¾ cups) Pumpkin Purée (see page 21)
150g (5oz/1½ cups) fresh cranberries
1 tbsp chopped rosemary leaves

Tip: The loaf freezes well for up to 3 months.

Preheat the oven to 190°C (170°C fan)/375°F/gas 5. Grease and line two 20 x 10cm (8 x 4 inch) loaf tins (pans) with baking parchment.

Put the flour, bicarbonate of soda, baking powder, salt and pumpkin spice mix in a bowl and mix well.

Using a stand food mixer or hand-held electric whisk, beat the butter and sugars until pale, light and fluffy. Beat in the eggs, one at a time, and then beat in the pumpkin purée.

Tip in the flour mixture and fold in gently. Lastly, stir in the whole cranberries and rosemary sprigs, distributing them throughout the mixture.

Divide between the lined loaf tins and level the tops. Bake for 55–60 minutes, or until well risen, golden brown and a thin skewer inserted in the centre comes out clean.

Leave the loaves in the tins for 10 minutes and then turn them out and cool on a wire rack. When cold, sprinkle with caster sugar and serve cut into slices.

Variations
• Top with pumpkin seeds.
• Add some chopped pecans or walnuts.
• Add some grated orange zest.
• Use frozen instead of fresh cranberries.

PUMPKIN SPICE POPPERS

//

Served fresh and piping hot from the oven, these warmly spiced popovers are a real treat for
all the family. Don't worry if you have some left over – just reheat in a preheated oven at 180°C
(160°C fan)/350°F/gas 4 for 5–10 minutes and they will crisp up nicely.

MAKES 6-12 POPPERS
PREP 10 MINUTES
COOK 30 MINUTES

125g (4½oz/1¼ cups) plain
   (all-purpose) flour
½ tsp sea salt
1 tsp Pumpkin Spice Mix
   (see page 15)
3 large free-range eggs
240ml (8fl oz/1 cup) milk
2 tbsp melted butter, plus extra
   for brushing

**PUMPKIN SPICE SUGAR
   COATING**
125g (4½oz/generous ½ cup)
   caster (superfine) sugar
1 tsp Pumpkin Spice Mix
   (see page 15)
4 tbsp melted unsalted butter

Preheat the oven to 220°C (200°C fan)/425°F/gas 7.

Sift the flour into a bowl and stir in the salt and pumpkin spice mix.

In another bowl, beat together the eggs, milk and melted butter
with a balloon whisk or hand-held electric whisk.

Gradually add the liquid mixture to the flour, stirring all the time,
until you have a smooth batter.

Place a 6-hole straight-sided popover pan or a 12-hole muffin
tin (pan) in the preheated oven for 5–10 minutes. Remove and
brush each cup with melted butter.

Quickly pour the batter into the cups and bake for 15 minutes.
Reduce the heat to 180°C (160°C fan)/350°F/gas 4 and bake
for a further 15 minutes, without opening the oven door, or until
well risen, crisp and golden brown.

Mix the sugar and pumpkin spice mix together on a plate. Brush
the warm popovers with melted butter and roll them in the spicy
sugar. Eat immediately while they are still hot and at their best.

Variations
· Add 2–3 teaspoons caster (superfine) sugar to the
  mixture.
· Add a few drops of vanilla extract.
· Drizzle with melted chocolate or salted caramel sauce.

SPICY PUMPKIN BLONDIES

//

These blondies are a cosy autumnal (fall) teatime treat. Like brownies, their darker cousins,
they have a crisp and chewy exterior and slightly soft centre.

MAKES 9 BLONDIES
PREP 20 MINUTES
COOK 25–30 MINUTES

100g (3½oz/½ cup) butter
115g (4oz/generous ½ cup)
   soft light brown sugar
2 free-range eggs
1 tsp vanilla extract
grated zest of 1 orange
115g (4oz/generous 1 cup) self-
   raising (self-rising) flour, sifted
3 tsp Pumpkin Spice Mix
   (see page 15)
115g (4oz/½ cup) Pumpkin Purée
   (see page 21)
200g (7oz/generous 1 cup)
   white chocolate chips
3 tbsp salted caramel sauce
   (optional)

Variations
- Add some chopped
  pecans or walnuts.
- Sprinkle the blondies
  with shredded
  coconut.

Preheat the oven to 190°C (170°C fan)/375°F/gas 5. Lightly
butter an 18cm (7 inch) square cake tin (baking pan) and line with
baking parchment.

Melt the butter in a saucepan set over a low heat and then stir
in the sugar. Increase the heat to medium and when the mixture
starts to colour and turn golden, remove from the heat.

Whisk the eggs, vanilla extract and orange zest in a large bowl and
then beat in the butter and sugar mixture. Gently fold in the flour
and pumpkin spice mix until everything is well combined, then
fold in half of the chocolate chips.

Transfer the mixture to the lined cake tin, spreading it out and
smoothing the top. If using, drop teaspoons of the salted caramel
sauce on top and then gently swirl into the cake mixture.

Bake for 20–25 minutes until well risen and golden and a skewer
inserted into the centre comes out nearly clean and only just
moist. Leave the cake in the tin until it's completely cold and then
cut into nine squares.

Bring a small pan of water to the boil and remove from the
heat. Put the remaining chocolate chips in a heatproof bowl and
suspend it over the pan without touching the water below. Stir
occasionally with a flat-bladed knife until they soften and melt.

Pour or drizzle the melted chocolate over the blondies and place
on a baking tray lined with baking parchment. Leave to cool until
set. Store in an airtight container for up to 3 days.

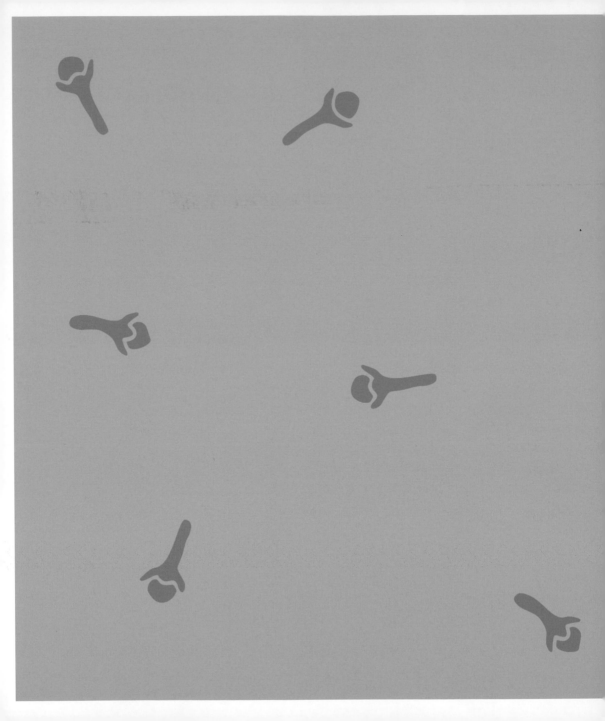

DRINKS

PUMPKIN-SPICED GOLDEN MILK

This warmly spiced, milky drink is relaxing and comforting at any time of the day. Adding pumpkin spice enhances its flavour and, what's more, it's dairy-free, gluten-free and anti-inflammatory.

SERVES 1
PREP 5 MINUTES
COOK 8–10 MINUTES

240ml (8fl oz/1 cup) reduced-fat coconut milk
1 tsp ground turmeric
½ tsp Pumpkin Spice Mix (see page 15), plus extra for dusting
¼ tsp ground ginger
a pinch of ground black pepper
1 cinnamon stick
2 cardamom pods, crushed (optional)
maple syrup, to taste

Tips: We've used reduced-fat tinned coconut milk, but you can use full-fat for a creamier drink.

For a pronounced pumpkin taste, also add 1 tablespoon Pumpkin Purée (see page 21).

Whisk the coconut milk, turmeric, pumpkin spice mix, ginger and black pepper until well combined and frothy. If wished, use a hand-held stick blender.

Transfer to a saucepan and add the cinnamon stick and crushed cardamom pods (if using). Bring to the boil, then reduce the heat to low and simmer gently for about 4–5 minutes, whisking once or twice.

Remove from the heat, remove the cinnamon stick and sweeten to taste with maple syrup. If using cardamon pods, strain the milk before whisking until frothy. Pour into a mug and, if wished, dust with more pumpkin spice mix.

Variations
- Use unsweetened almond milk instead of coconut milk.
- Add the seeds of ½ vanilla pod (bean).
- If you don't like maple syrup, use sugar or stevia.
- Add ½ teaspoon grated fresh root ginger but you'll need to strain the milk before drinking it.

PUMPKIN-SPICED HOT CHOCOLATE

///

Warm up on a cold night with a mug of this soothing hot chocolate spiked with pumpkin purée and spice mix. To transform it into something super special, you could add a dash of whisky or cognac.

SERVES 2
PREP 5 MINUTES
COOK 5 MINUTES

120ml (4fl oz/½ cup) milk
85ml (3fl oz/generous ¼ cup) double (heavy) cream
45g (1½oz/¼ cup) dark (bittersweet) chocolate chips
1 tsp unsweetened cocoa powder
1–2 tbsp Pumpkin Purée (see page 21)
½ tsp Pumpkin Spice Mix (see page 15)
½ tsp vanilla extract
whipped cream and grated or shaved chocolate, to serve

Put the milk, cream, chocolate chips and cocoa powder in a saucepan set over a low to medium heat. Whisk until the chocolate melts and the mixture is well blended and smooth.

Add 1 tablespoon pumpkin purée and then the pumpkin spice mix and stir well. Taste and add more pumpkin purée if you prefer a more intense flavour. Stir in the vanilla extract.

When the chocolate mixture is hot (but not boiling), pour it into two small mugs or heatproof glasses. Decorate with whipped cream and sprinkle some chocolate over the top. Serve immediately.

Variations
· Dust with pumpkin spice mix, grated nutmeg or ground cinnamon.
· Substitute white or milk chocolate chips for dark.
· Sprinkle with grated orange zest.

PUMPKIN SPICED LATTE MILKSHAKE

//

Here's a delicious milkshake to brighten up chilly autumnal (fall) days. It's so quick and easy to prepare and it makes a refreshing change from hot lattes. If you don't have an espresso machine or moka pot, just substitute some freshly brewed strong coffee.

SERVES 2
PREP 10 MINUTES

240ml (8fl oz/1 cup) milk
2 tbsp Pumpkin Purée (see page 21)
1 tsp Pumpkin Spice Mix (see page 15), plus extra for dusting
4 shots espresso (or 2 pods)
1 tsp vanilla extract
300g (10oz/2 cups) coffee ice cream
whipped cream and cinnamon sticks, to serve

Put the milk, pumpkin purée, pumpkin spice mix, espresso, vanilla and ice cream in a blender. Blitz until smooth.

Divide between two tall glasses and top with some whipped cream and a dusting of pumpkin spice mix. Serve immediately, garnished with cinnamon sticks.

Tip: You can use dairy-free milk, such as oat or soya milk, to make this milkshake but the result may be less thick and creamy.

Variations
· Use vanilla instead of coffee ice cream.
· Drizzle with Pumpkin Spice Syrup (see page 18) or salted caramel sauce.
· Add some ice cubes.
· If wished, sweeten with maple syrup.

PUMPKIN SPICE PROTEIN SHAKE

///

You can whisk up this milkshake in less than 5 minutes, making it a great way to start the day for people on-the-go. This health shake is high in protein and is the perfect pick-me-up after a workout as well as a nutritious breakfast.

SERVES 1
PREP 5 MINUTES

240ml (8fl oz/1 cup) cold unsweetened almond milk
1 frozen banana, sliced
3 tbsp Pumpkin Purée (see page 21)
1 x 30g (1oz) scoop vanilla protein powder
1 tbsp nut butter, e.g. almond or cashew
½ tsp Pumpkin Spice Mix (see page 15), plus extra for dusting
a few drops of vanilla extract
ice cubes, to serve (optional)

Put all the ingredients in a blender and blitz until smooth.

Pour into a tall glass, add some ice cubes (if wished) and dust with pumpkin spice mix. Enjoy.

Tip: Adding a frozen banana to a milkshake or smoothie makes it thicker and creamier. Before freezing bananas, always peel them and cut into thick slices or chunks. Freeze overnight in a plastic bag. This makes it easier to add them to smoothies so you won't need to use a heavy-duty blender.

Variations
· Use peanut butter for a stronger flavour.
· Use oat or even coconut milk instead of almond milk.
· Add some plain Greek yoghurt or a scoop of vanilla ice cream.
· Add a couple of chopped Medjool dates.
· If using plain protein powder, sweeten with honey or maple syrup.
· Or use chocolate protein powder.

PUMPKIN SPICE MARTINI

//

Who would have thought of adding pumpkin spice mix to a cocktail, but this creamy vodka martini, served shaken, not stirred, tastes delicious. Try it and see for yourself! If you're going to sugar the rim, you will need to use a real martini glass.

SERVES 1
PREP 10 MINUTES
CHILL 10–15 MINUTES

ice cubes
45ml (1½fl oz) shot (jigger) vodka
45ml (1½fl oz) shot (jigger)
    pumpkin spice liqueur
45ml (1½fl oz) shot (jigger)
    Baileys or other Irish cream
    liqueur
¼ tsp Pumpkin Spice Mix
    (see page 15)
freshly grated nutmeg, to serve

PUMPKIN SPICE SUGAR
50g (2oz/¼ cup) caster
    (superfine) sugar
1 tbsp Pumpkin Spice Mix
    (see page 15)

Make the pumpkin spice sugar for the rim of the glass: mix together the sugar and pumpkin spice mix and transfer to a large saucer. Pour some cold water into another saucer.

Take a martini glass and, holding it upside down, quickly dip the rim into the cold water and then into the spiced sugar. Place the glass in the freezer for 10–15 minutes until frosted and chilled.

Fill a cocktail shaker with ice cubes and add the vodka, pumpkin spice liqueur, Baileys and pumpkin spice mix.

Cover and shake vigorously for 10 seconds or until the metal shaker looks frosty.

Strain into the chilled and frosted martini glass and dust with a little grated nutmeg. Serve immediately.

Variations
- Use vanilla vodka to add more flavour.
- To make the cocktail sweeter, add 1 tablespoon sugar syrup or Pumpkin Spice Syrup (see page 18).
- Serve with a cinnamon stick or even some whipped cream on top.

MULLED WINE WITH PUMPKIN SPICE

//

For many of us, a glass of mulled wine is the taste of Christmas. Serve it to family and friends as a warming, welcoming drink. It's perfect for festive and New Year's Eve parties. If possible, pour the hot mulled wine into a jug to serve and use heatproof glasses with long stems or handles.

**MAKES ABOUT 2 LITRES
(3½ PINTS/8 CUPS)
PREP 5 MINUTES
COOK 20 MINUTES**

2 oranges
1 lemon
2 cinnamon sticks
6 whole cloves
1 tsp whole allspice berries
2–3 tsp Pumpkin Spice Mix
    (see page 15)
115g (4oz/½ cup) white sugar
300ml (½ pint/1¼ cups) water
2 x 750ml (25fl oz) bottles
    full-bodied fruity red wine
100ml (3½fl oz/scant ½ cup)
    brandy, rum or port (optional)

Peel a large strip of rind off one of the oranges and another strip off the lemon. Place in a large saucepan with the cinnamon, cloves, allspice berries and pumpkin spice mix. Add the sugar, water and red wine and set over a low to medium heat.

Stir gently until the sugar dissolves, then continue to heat thoroughly for 15 minutes – taking care not to allow it to boil – until the spicy flavours develop and infuse the wine.

Cut the lemon and oranges into thin slices. Add to the mulled wine with the brandy, rum or port (if using) and simmer for 5 more minutes.

Ladle the hot mulled wine into heatproof glasses to serve.

Tip: Stud a whole orange with the cloves and add to the pan. Its flavours will infuse the liquid and it will look pretty when you serve it.

Variations
- Add ground ginger or grated fresh root ginger tied up in a muslin (cheesecloth) bag.
- Add a star anise or cardamom pods or even a stalk of lemongrass.
- Substitute light muscovado sugar for the white sugar.

PUMPKIN SPICE LATTE

//

There's no need to visit a coffee shop or café when you can make a delicious latte at home, flavoured with pumpkin spice. If you're planning on making this regularly, it's worth investing in a hand-held milk frother for a more professional result.

SERVES 1
PREP 5 MINUTES
COOK 5 MINUTES

240ml (8fl oz/1 cup) dairy
   or non-dairy milk
2 shots espresso (or 1 pod)
2 tbsp Pumpkin Purée
   (see page 21)
½ tsp Pumpkin Spice Mix
   (see page 15), plus extra
   for dusting
1–2 tbsp maple syrup, to taste
1 tsp vanilla extract
whipped cream, to serve
   (optional)

Heat the milk, espresso, pumpkin purée, pumpkin spice, maple syrup and vanilla in a saucepan set over a medium heat – do not allow to boil. Whisk or froth with a hand-held milk frother until warmed through and frothy.

Transfer to a mug, pouring the frothed milk slowly and steadily from a relatively high position. The milk should pour first with the froth at the end as you lower the pan towards the mug.

Serve immediately, topped with whipped cream (if using) and a dusting of pumpkin spice mix. Enjoy!

Tips: If you don't have a hand-held milk frother, you can use an electric one or a plunger-type frother.

Any non-dairy milk will work well – try unsweetened almond or soya, coconut or oat milk.

If you don't have an espresso machine or pot, use 120ml (4fl oz/½ cup) cafetière or strong instant coffee.

Variations
· Drizzle with some Pumpkin Spice Syrup (see page 18).
· Garnish with a cinnamon stick.
· Substitute sugar for the maple syrup.

KETO PUMPKIN SPICE LATTE

//

This keto latte is quick and easy to make. If you're using store-bought pumpkin purée rather than homemade, check the label and make sure it's sugar-free.

SERVES 1
PREP 5 MINUTES
COOK 5 MINUTES

240ml (8fl oz/1 cup)
   unsweetened almond milk
2 tbsp sugar-free Pumpkin Purée
   (see page 21)
⅛ tsp Pumpkin Spice Mix
   (see page 15), plus extra
   for dusting
1–2 tbsp erythritol
½ tsp vanilla extract
1 tsp coconut oil
2 shots hot espresso (or 1 pod)
whipped cream, to serve

Put the milk, pumpkin purée, pumpkin spice, erythritol, vanilla and coconut oil in a blender and blitz until well combined.

Transfer to a saucepan set over a medium heat – do not allow to boil. Whisk or froth with a hand-held milk frother until warmed through and frothy.

Put the hot espresso in a mug and pour in the warm milk mixture. Blend and froth in the mug with a small hand-held milk frother.

Serve immediately, topped with whipped cream and a dusting of pumpkin spice mix. Enjoy!

Variations
- Use unsalted butter or ghee instead of coconut oil.
- Sprinkle with freshly grated nutmeg or a pinch of ground cinnamon.
- Omit the vanilla and use unsweetened vanilla almond milk.
- You can use monk fruit sweetener instead of erythritol.

INDEX

//

INDEX